C000229380

Women and Men Af

Women and Men
After Christendom

The Dis-Ordering of Gender Relationships

Fran Porter

Paternoster:
thinking faith

26 25 24 23 22 21 20 19 18 17 16 15   12 11 10 9 8 7 6 5 4 3 2 1

First published 2015 by Paternoster
Paternoster is an imprint of Authentic Media Limited
52 Presley Way, Crownhill, Milton Keynes, MK8 0ES.
authenticmedia.co.uk

British Library Cataloguing in Publication Data

A catalogue record for this book is available from the British Library

ISBN 978-1-84227-759-1
978-1-84227-905-2 (e-book)

Cover Design by David McNeill (revocreative.co.uk)
Printed and bound by CPI Group (UK) Ltd., Croydon, CR0 4YY

Contents

Series Preface: *After Christendom*

Christendom was a historical era, a geographical region, a political arrangement, a sacral culture and an ideology. For many centuries Europeans have lived in a society that was nominally Christian. Church and state have been the pillars of a remarkable civilisation that can be traced back to the decision of the emperor Constantine I early in the fourth century to replace paganism with Christianity as the imperial religion.

Christendom, a brilliant but brutal culture, flourished in the Middle Ages, fragmented in the reformation of the sixteenth century, but persisted despite the onslaught of modernity. While exporting its values and practices to other parts of the world, however, it has been slowly declining during the past three centuries. In the twenty-first century Christendom is unravelling.

What will emerge from the demise of Christendom is not yet clear, but we can now describe much of western culture as 'post-Christendom'.

Post-Christendom is the culture that emerges as the Christian faith loses coherence within a society that has been definitively shaped by the Christian story and as the institutions that have been developed to express Christian convictions decline in influence.

This definition, proposed and unpacked in *Post-Christendom**, the first book in the 'After Christendom' series, has gained widespread acceptance. *Post-Christendom* investigated the Christendom legacy and raised numerous issues that are explored in the rest of the series. The authors of this series, who write from within the Anabaptist tradition, see the current challenges facing the church not as the loss of a golden age but as opportunities to recover a more biblical and more Christian way of being God's people in God's world.

The series addresses a wide range of issues, including social and political engagement, how we read Scripture, youth work, mission, worship and the shape and ethos of the church after Christendom.

Books already published:

Stuart Murray: *Post-Christendom*
Stuart Murray: *Church after Christendom*
Jonathan Bartley: *Faith and Politics after Christendom*
Jo & Nigel Pimlott: *Youth Work after Christendom*
Alan & Eleanor Kreider: *Worship and Mission after Christendom*
Lloyd Pietersen: *Reading the Bible after Christendom*
Andrew Francis: *Hospitality and Community after Christendom*

These books are not intended to be the last word on the subjects they address, but an invitation to discussion and further exploration. Additional material, including extracts from published books and information about future volumes, can be found at anabaptistnetwork.com/After-Christendom.

Stuart Murray

---
* Stuart Murray: *Post-Christendom; church and mission in a strange new world* (Carlisle: Paternoster, 2004), 19.

Foreword

In a post-Christendom era many Christians face the issue of how women and men should relate to one another. Assumptions and patterns of behavior that for centuries seemed obvious to Christians have crumbled. Christians today have lost power and credibility. But the Christian faith still appeals to others when Christians live in ways that are truthful and convey hope.

In *Women and Men After Christendom*, Fran Porter makes a contribution to our time that is learned, buoyant and full of hope. Her background has prepared her ideally for the task. She is a researcher, writer and teacher with degrees in theology and in women's studies, and has written several publications on gender, pluralism and faith. She has a deep knowledge of gender studies and a lively appreciation of the contribution of feminist scholars. She has done unique research, listening to women in a conflicted late-Christendom society (Northern Ireland) as they reflect on their lives and relationships. She is a committed Christian who loves the church, whatever its failings, and has a special concern for reconciliation. She is our friend, whom we esteem deeply.

This is in some ways a hard time to be a Christian but, in other ways, it is a bracing and exciting time. In post-Christendom we must make reassessments. We must re-examine Christian history; listen anew to Jesus Christ and his good news; and chart ways forward that enable Christians, in a world we cannot control, to live and speak distinctively. In these ways, we Christians can contribute to the shalom of the world, particularly in the crucial area of the relationship between women and men.

In order to make this contribution, Christians must face into obstacles. One of these is the way that Christians have told their story. *The Handbook of Christianity: A Lion Handbook* (1990) highlights the problem. Its index of 'people' lists 1,210 names, but only thirty-five of the 'people' were women. Why? It is not that women had made no contributions to the Christian story; the Handbook's editors knew better than that, and today they would augment the thirty-five women with many others. But the Handbook was evidence of the durable reality of patriarchalism, a system that had come into being that diminishes women, prohibits them as teachers, ignores them as writers, and when they make contributions simply looks the other way. Of course, patriarchalism was already present in the early centuries of the church. But with the coming of Christendom in the fourth and fifth centuries, male Christian leaders solidified patriarchalism in the church's hierarchal institutions. Further, Christian theologians rationalized the exclusion of women, dismissing them as deficient and dangerous. So when women did important things – in families, monasteries, renewal movements – it didn't matter. Women were peripheral and marginal. Their contributions were lightweight. And so when Christians told their story across the centuries, it was a story of 'a no (wo)mans land' (Christine Trevett). Patriarchalism is alive today; and its costs for both women and men, and for the credibility of the Christian message are incalculable.

In the pages of this book, Fran Porter serves us all by locating contemporary issues about women and men within the long sweep of Christian history. Her treatment of the solidification of patriarchy in early Christendom is telling. Patriarchy is a system, not of the common humanity that Christians share in Christ, but of a broken humanity that asserts the power of men over women. Fran grieves as she notes Christians arguing that, because women are deficient and dangerous, they must be submissive to men. She notes the suffering of women across Christian history, and notes its cumulative effects – century after century – in magisterial Protestant as well as Catholic societies, and in the 'free churches' as well. Fran has particular insight into ways Christians have used the Bible to silence women and keep them subservient.

But Fran is convinced that there is good news for women and men, even now in post-Christendom. Her faith and hope are rooted in Jesus. Fran sees the incarnation as God's unique self-disclosure, and she sees Jesus challenging maleness as normative humanity. She is fascinated by his sense of new possibilities with the advent of God's kingdom; and is intrigued by the ways he redefined family as those who do God's will and those whom he calls his friends. She is intrigued by the way Jesus refused to behave as a competitive male.

She also writes confidently about 'the practices of the first churches', including those founded by Paul. This points to a characteristic of Fran's work that we find valuable: her confidence that the Bible speaks good news, even in some of its 'hard passages'. For example, the Pauline text of 1 Timothy 2:8–15. We may wonder, can anything good come out of a passage that suggests that women should be silent? Fran finds life even here. She points out that, counter-culturally for his time, Paul insists that

women should 'learn', and further that 'silence' (*hesuchia*) is an attitude
that Paul recommends for men as well as women. It means calm self-control!

Fran is an equally sensitive guide to the issues of gender that preoc-
cupy Christians today. She understands the contemporary debates about
'complementarianism' and equality; she shows how patriarchalism has
functioned and lives on in many Christian traditions; she knows how
feminist and non-feminist Christians use the Bible; she understands the
concerns of men as well as of women. In all these, her insights come not
just from her wide reading but also from her good listening. Fran is especially insightful when she shows why the Christa sculptures and female
God-language, though scandalous to some, are helpful to her and many
others. She also is winsomely insistent that gifting, not gender, is central
to the calling and roles of Christians. Women and men must all be free to
teach, lead, care for the weak and make tea. And no one, in a movement
that acknowledges Jesus Christ as Lord, may function through competition, power and control.

As Fran looks forward into the world after Christendom, she is confi-
dent. We Christians, women and men, from now on will have to witness
to the gospel by the way we live, not by the power we wield. Jesus will
help us in our witness. As we women and men rediscover his teaching
and way, we will find that peacemaking and reconciliation become
central to our lives. We will know a restoration of relationship to God
when we allow God to restore our relations with other humans. And, in a
theme that recurs in her book, we, women and men, will become friends
– friends of each other and friends of Jesus who has called us his friends.

Eleanor Kreider and Alan Kreider
Elkhart, Indiana
March 25, 2014

Acknowledgements

My thanks are due to those who have supported me in producing this book. In particular, I would like to thank Stuart Murray for trusting me with this project and for patiently waiting for its completion. Stuart, along with Linda Wilson, Alan Kreider, Paula Gooder and Veronica Zundel, have read and commented on parts of the manuscript at various stages and I remain very grateful for their insights, expertise and encouragements. My thanks, too, go to Mike Parsons at Paternoster who has been enthusiastic about this book from the beginning. It was my pleasure to work with Trisha Dale as copy-editor of the manuscript, which has benefitted from her thoroughness and skill. I am greatly indebted to Eleanor Kreider and Alan Kreider whose generous foreword is a reflection of their generous lives; I consider myself privileged to know them. Finally, as always, my thanks and love to David (he who inhabits the smaller study) whose love and presence makes so much possible for me that would otherwise remain elusive.

Abbreviations

CUP   Cambridge University Press
DLT   Darton, Longman & Todd
IVP   Inter-Varsity Press
JBL   *Journal of Biblical Literature*
LGBT lesbian, gay, bisexual and transgender
OUP   Oxford University Press
UP   University Press
YUP   Yale University Press

Introduction

I moved house recently. In this new house, my husband and I each have our own room. We have taken the two smaller bedrooms and made them both into studies. One of these rooms is bigger than the other – not by very much, but obviously so on opening the doors. I have the bigger study.

We had a removal firm help us with the move. The team of three men moved our desks into our respective rooms, brought in the bookcases, lining up the furniture where we asked, and then began bringing in the boxes of books, papers and computer equipment. I stood at the top of the stairs indicating which carefully labelled box should be taken into which room.

Part way through these 'box runs', one of the team came out of my room and asked me, without any humour, irony, sarcasm, hint of friendly banter, or cheek, 'Why do you have the bigger study?' This was a highly gendered question. His question was not so much one of curiosity as it was of bafflement. Something clearly did not add up for him, and despite his otherwise professional manner, he was compelled to cross the boundary into asking for a justification of our choice of room allocation.

Somewhat taken aback, I gave a highly gendered answer. I did indeed attempt to justify the situation, and in doing so accepted his assumption that there was something about this arrangement that was questionable. So, rather than replying with another question, 'Why shouldn't I?', I simply said that I worked from home so spent more time in my home study and that my husband had an office at work. In other words, in terms of square footage, he had the larger space than me, albeit in two locations. I was giving reassurance, not to worry, all is in order in the world, just as it should be, with of course the man having the greater space.

All of us live lives impacted by gendered thinking and structures, however much – or little – we are aware of this. This book is about gender – about how women and men relate together. It consciously explores historical, theological and social influences that have shaped the social relations between women and men.

While I was finishing writing this book I had a conversation with a 19-year-old student. He was finding his chosen course of study frustrating because he felt it was focused on how to get a job in his field rather than the 'whys and wherefores' of his subject. Something of a self-taught philosopher, he was interested in the bigger picture that he felt was missing. He told me about life as a student, some of the things that had brought him to this point, and what he hoped he might do in the future.

He then asked me what I did when I left school. I briefly outlined what had brought me to the point of being involved in social and theological research and some of the things I had done. 'Do you have faith yourself?', he wanted to know. I replied yes, I was a Christian and so I was an 'insider' to much of the work I did. His response was immediate: 'But don't you find Christianity *really* offensive to women?'

I asked him to tell me what had led him to say this. He was very clear. Men wrote the Bible to tell women what to do, to keep them unequal. And that was what all religion was – it was about controlling people, keeping them in their place. In his sharp critique of what he thought about Christianity, he summed up the focus of this book, which is looking at the relationship of women and men in the light of the shift to post-Christendom.

The term 'post-Christendom shift' refers to how we are moving away from a situation where the church has religious, social and political power which can be imposed upon others to one in which Christians witness to the gospel by the way they live, not by the power they wield. This book is concerned with what this new understanding and practice might mean for relationships between women and men, which throughout Christendom have followed a hierarchically ordered gender pattern. The dis-ordering of the book's subtitle is not about advocating chaos, but about dismantling this pattern of male dominance and female subordination.

While the transition to post-Christendom may at times feel disorienting as the church and Christians are dislocated from a privileged centre in society to a more marginal and peripheral status, it is also an opportunity to re-imagine ourselves differently. This is no less so in terms of the social relations between women and men. Can considering this age-old conversation in the emerging light of a post-Christendom framework offer us fresh or renewed insight?

In this re-imagining, I share with the student the pull of the bigger picture. Therefore, this is not so much a 'how to' book, but a 'why we should' book. It does not provide models to follow, but seeks to expose the nature of the challenge. This is partly because understanding something of the dynamics of Christendom's gender hierarchy is necessary if we are to move beyond it, if we are to have more than superficial attempts to live as women and men after Christendom. And it is partly because I believe such living will look different depending on particular situations. A witness to re-imagined relationships will involve diversity as much as it does innovation. This diversity itself will be an implicit challenge to the highly restrictive gender order bound up in Christendom thinking and behaving.

So imprinted on us is a Christendom order of gender that the first difficulty we face is trying to think outside of its constraints. To help us to do this, and to remove ambiguity over some of the terms used in this book, Chapter 1 begins with making plain a number of contexts in which our consideration takes place. It introduces the breadth of the notion of Christendom and the importance of its integral idea of order, which I am challenging in this book. It notes how patriarchy – which includes a hierarchy of males over females – is enmeshed within Christendom; hence, the ethos of empire is sustained by women's subordination. A discussion of the terms sex and gender, and sexuality, affirms the value of our embodiment as women and men while highlighting the way sexual distinction has been used to structure inequality in terms of belief, value and behaviour.

The chapter finishes with a note on hermeneutics, which I use both in a broad and more particular sense in this book. Broadly speaking, hermeneutics is about the framework we use for interpreting our world; a Christendom framework is one of a divinely ordered hierarchy (the word hierarchy comes from the Greek *hieros* meaning sacred and *arche* meaning rule). This contrasts with the frameworks of equality and friendship that are discussed in later chapters. In a more specific sense, biblical hermeneutics is about how we interpret the Bible, crucial for any discussion on gender relationships. But centuries of being told that the Scriptures prescribe patriarchal gender norms have left us unable to see that the biblical narratives actually contain challenges to such norms.

Chapter 2, therefore, explores the New Testament, both gospels and epistles, to tease out an unfolding narrative of groups of believers who were wrestling with the impact of their experiences on their social and political relations, including that of gender. The patriarchy of the world before Christendom was entangled with the Roman Empire (as it would be with the Christian empire that followed). The Christian claim, therefore, of belonging to a new community in God, rather than identifying with family, religious, political or national allegiances, was disturbing to the existing social and indeed sacral order. It questioned the usual social conventions of marriage, kin and household that structured the lives of women and men, particularly in the light of the expected imminent return of Jesus. The image of God as father was a direct challenge to the place of all patriarchs, whether in kin networks, households, or as heads of states. Its significance is not as a male as opposed to female metaphor, but as a picture that confounds systems of domination. A challenge in the world of the first Christians, it has the potential to continue to be a challenge to Christendom thinking, both past and present.

The chapter traces some of the diversity among believers in the first churches as they adjusted to the realities of a prolonged period of living in 'the last days' in the midst of mainstream society and culture, which, of course, had nurtured and formed them before their encounter with Christ. The emerging organizational structures of the church developed in the second and third centuries to a dominant patriarchal pattern, but not without well-attested counter traditions. Such counter traditions continued throughout the Christendom period, despite various attempts to obscure them.

It is the impact of Christendom on the relationship between women and men that I turn to in Chapter 3. Whatever his motivation, the decision of the emperor Constantine at the start of the fourth century to favour Christianity within his empire not only brought an end to the persecution previously experienced by the church. It also began a realignment of Christianity from the margins to the centre of the state and its power. To help illustrate the enormity of this change, I begin the chapter with a broader view of the impact of this mainstreaming of Christianity in the empire, including how religious orthodoxy became enforced with the power of the state. I then look at three dynamics through which the enmeshment of the church with the trappings of empire impacted on gender relations.

The first of these is the solidifying of the division between clergy and laity, with an increasing move to a priesthood that was not only male, but also celibate, and one that church authorities put much energy and law into enforcing. This spiritual and social hierarchy between clerics and laity relied on and reinforced negative and detrimental views of women – their physicality and their intellectual and moral capacities, for even celibate living was insufficient to bestow on women the purity that would enable them to serve at the altar. Second, the chapter considers the impact of the Reformation's understanding of the relationship between family, church and state. The Reformers' renegotiation of the relationship between sexuality and holiness that saw them closing convents and monasteries and promoting clerical marriage was imbued with patriarchal ideology. Marriages, and particularly those of the clergy, became 'the showcase of Christian living',[1] and foundational to this was the authoritative role of the father in the household, which in turn was viewed as an analogy of the state. Women or men stepping outside of accepted patterns were considered disorderly and a threat to society's wellbeing.

Chapter 3 finishes looking at a third dynamic underpinning the first two: Christian understandings of sex and sexuality. In particular, the double standard inherent in much Christian sexual ethics not only has seen women more associated than men with humanity's sexual nature, but also viewed them as more culpable than men for humanity's sexual failings. The outworking of this dynamic may have presented itself differently over the centuries, but sexual ethics remains core to Christian self-understanding up to the present day. It is possible to see contemporary churches' struggles to maintain more traditional structuring of relations between women and men as attempts to maintain a distinctive Christian identity in the context of their declining power and influence in a post-Christendom world.

Chapter 4 considers a more recent and continuing response to patriarchal and Christendom gender order – the discourse of equality. Equality is a framework for envisioning the relationship between women and men that does not put them in subordinate and dominant positions. Rather, it challenges the values and the practices that perpetuate such arrangements, whether in domestic settings or public institutions. To survey the progress in equality that women have gained in various ways in the twentieth century is to realize that gains have come slowly and been imperfectly implemented. Failure to address the deeper ways that gender inequality is structured in both personal and public life has inhibited greater equality while at the same time giving a general impression that sufficient equality has been achieved. However, among other achievements, women's movements have succeeded in putting male behaviour and privilege under a spotlight. The response to this has been an identifiable men's movement, including a spectrum from the therapeutic mythopoeticism of *Iron John*[2] to pro-feminist White Ribbon campaigns that focus on ending male violence against women.

Christian responses to the contemporary context of equality are dominated by the discourse of the feminization of the church. This chapter explores this conversation and the responses, epitomized by the Promise Keepers in the USA, that focus on how men might be engaged in Christian and church life. It suggests that the opportunities for personal growth that men are experiencing (and their female partners are often valuing) through such responses should not stop a more in-depth critical analysis of the discourse of feminization. A historical perspective on so-called feminization enables us to see how, from the eighteenth century, patriarchy has been adapting through various social changes, re-inventing itself but keeping a gender hierarchy intact, despite rhetoric to the contrary. The chapter concludes that equality is a demanding ethic, both personally and socially and, while perhaps not the most natural language for theology, one that finds resonance with the life of Jesus and the practice of the first churches.

It is theological imagination that is thought about in Chapter 5. The sense we make of the transcendent reality of God in our lives shapes our human communities. This is no less so for gender relations. When we say that humanity is made in the image of God but the chief human images we draw on to picture God are male, while at the same time finding it deeply disturbing, for example, to refer to God as 'she', this has implications for the relationship between women and men. Our gender-exclusive language reveals what is often denied, that we situate femaleness differently to maleness in terms of the relationship to deity, and this has implications for how women and men are situated with each other. Our theological imagination determines our social gender relations.

Of course, the unique image of God we have is Jesus, and Chapter 5 goes on to ask what meaning we are to take from the fact that Jesus was male. Contrary to much focus on the significance of Jesus' sex, I suggest the key question here is not whether God could have become incarnate as a woman. Rather, it is whether there is anything about women and femaleness that means they are not suitable to image the divine. I explore this question through reflecting on responses to encountering artistic portrayals of a crucified Christ in female form. The visceral reactions that such representations provoke tell us much about the underlying symbolism that structures our theology and our gendered social organization.

The crucified Christ, of course, has a central place within Christian tradition. Here too, theological imagination has had a profound impact on how women and men relate. Frequently, Jesus' submission to his own suffering has been used to encourage or coerce women to accept the suffering and injustice they encounter – not least from male abuse and violence, but also from patriarchal social systems that treat women unfairly – rather than to challenge it. Finally, therefore, Chapter 5 revisits the meaning of the cross, suggesting that its role in endorsing suffering cannot be accounted for simply as a perversion of Christian theology. Such meaning derived from the death of Christ is, rather, imbued with the legacy of Christendom understandings of atonement, which developed in the medieval period when cross and sword combined to coerce Christian political and religious allegiance.

The focus of Chapter 6 is on the Bible and in particular the New Testament. The overwhelming tendency has been to understand gender

relations on the basis of a select number of New Testament verses, sometimes called the 'hard passages'. In contrast to this contracted approach, I
suggest an expansive threefold way of reading the New Testament when
thinking about the relation between women and men. First, this means
letting the whole text inform our understanding of gender relations.
This involves making gender visible where it has been absent from our
reading and discovering about gender relations in unexpected places.
Second, it means bearing in mind the breadth of church life, experience
and dialogue that we meet in the New Testament and joining in that
conversation ourselves. These two approaches provide the context for
the third way of reading that I suggest, which is a close-up look at the
so-called 'hard passages'. These verses remain important to explore, but
through engaging in an expansive approach to New Testament reading,
we open ourselves up to new encounters with these texts.

In effect, Chapter 2 consists of the first two approaches so in Chapter
6 I focus on the third approach, illustrating it by considering 1 Timothy
2:8–15. These verses have been used as the definitive, authoritative
verdict confirming women's subordination but, as I demonstrate, it is not
only possible but more plausible to read them differently.

In the light of centuries of gender relations that have been characterized by antagonism, I suggest, in Chapter 7, that we use the notion of
friendship to think of women and men, not just or even primarily as
individuals, but as a paradigm for thinking about humanity as female
and male. By drawing on ancient practices of friendship – which contrast
with contemporary ones, but which also are partially subverted to new
ends in the New Testament – I propose this motif offers us a qualitatively
different approach to a Christendom mindset of power and control.

Finally, I return to the bigger picture with which I began and a reminder
of how Christendom's patriarchal gender order shapes all our lives. I do
so with the hope that Christian communities, in grasping the importance
of giving attention to gender, will creatively engage in their own dis-
ordering of gender relationships.

1.

Thinking Beyond Christendom's Gender

When Kate Middleton married Prince William in 2011 many media commentators talked about how this was a very modern couple; in particular, Kate did not promise to obey in her marriage vows. Yet this 'modern' marriage was caught up in a very old custom that puts women secondary to men. For, at the time of their marriage, while Prince William remained heir to the throne, second in line after his father Prince Charles, should the Duke and Duchess of Cambridge have had a first-born daughter, the royal line would have passed not to her as a girl, but to any younger brother. This principle of male primogeniture (where younger brothers succeed, in this case, to the throne before an older sister) seems anachronistic in the current era of equality. So much so that, by the time their first child (as it turned out, a boy) was born in July 2013, British law had been changed to allow a first-born daughter to succeed to the British crown even if she had a younger brother.[1]

Putting aside for the moment any symbolic value, it might be argued that, in a parliamentary democracy with a constitutional monarchy, the overturning of a quaint custom of male privilege to the throne has little impact on the rest of us. However, the thinking and structures of the gender hierarchy undergirding the notion and practice of primogeniture are the common heritage for all of us. Society has increasingly wrestled with matters of equal pay, equal standing before the law, access to education and employment, and the way we relate as women and men in our homes and workplaces, raise families, and participate in society.

In contemporary society we have a public rhetoric of sex equality while living with the imperfection of its implementation and arguments about its application. Churches, however, are removed from the remit of equality legislation, claiming a different and higher authority, which has allowed them to exclude women from priesthood or leadership roles. Varying justifications are used: arguments about women's and men's natures that make men suitable for leadership in a way that women are not; that only men can represent the divine because implicitly maleness speaks of divinity in a way that femaleness does not; that a spiritual equality is not the same as a functional equality and God has given us the order of male leadership; or even on the basis of tradition – that is has (allegedly) ever been so.

Alongside these questions about rule and authority are debates about the use of inclusive language for worshipping communities and for the divine, and about the participation and contribution of women generally in church life while observing the decline in attendance by men. Bound up in all of this is the notion of the feminization of the church, which is said to be becoming a feminine environment at the expense of masculine involvement. At the same time, churches continue to voice within their own communities and to wider society views about social and familial roles for women and men. In doing so, they appeal to a Judeo-Christian tradition which, while adapted to living in a modern market economy, frequently is cited as affirming a traditional pattern of biologically determined, and hence differentiated, social function. All of these conversations are about gender relations.

The challenge to, and renegotiation of, accepted norms and patterns of being and behaviour for women and men evident in the past one hundred years has been occurring alongside a decline in Christian influence in society and a move away from the Christendom model of Christians in the world. This book brings these two transitions together – gender relations in a post-Christendom society.

Christendom was characterized by a particular kind of order. This order was an alignment between God, empire and church that was imposed and enforced by state and ecclesial officials. Typical of all systems of domination and subordination, dissent was not allowed. Power and authority were vested in emperors not their subjects, in clergy not the laity, and in men and not women. The gradual shift to post-Christendom has seen this hier-archical ordering of relationships increasingly challenged. This book focuses on women and men after Christendom. What does our understanding of what is happening in the post-Christendom shift – in the move away from hierarchically ordered and imposed power – mean for gender relationships?

We face a difficulty in thinking about this because so much of our practice of gender is unreflective – it is just the way things are, embedded in our social organization, with gendered mind-sets and structures reinforcing each other. What we think affects how we behave while our experiences lead us to believe certain things about women and men. We have a tendency to assume that because something is replicated all around us it must be inevi-table. The fact that things have always been a certain way leads on to the idea that they are natural and right. We focus on under-standing how women and men may better relate and understand one another on the basis of a particular gendered framework of understanding, without asking if things need to be this way, if we want them to be like this, or if they could be different.

Yet the confusing and often confused debates we have about women and men reflect the difficulties we have of thinking beyond Christendom's gender – of thinking beyond a hierarchical and oppositional divide between women and men (which is the way gender has been viewed from the time of Aristotle). In this gender divide, women and men are set against one another and often in a power struggle, which for centuries was won by men and more recently has seen women finding ways of countering male dominance. The transition to post-Christendom, with all its reassessments, is an opportunity to think afresh about the social relations of women and men.

In exploring these matters, I am using a number of concepts that it is useful to clarify: Christendom and post-Christendom; the notion of order; patriarchy; sex and gender; sexuality; and hermeneutics.

Christendom and After

What do we mean by Christendom and post-Christendom? Stuart Murray summarizes, 'Christendom was a historical era, a geographical region, a political arrangement, a sacral culture and an ideology.'[2] He expands this the following ways:

- Christendom was a geographical region in which almost everyone was at least nominally Christian.
- Christendom was a historical era resulting from the fourth-century conversion of Constantine and lasting into the late twentieth century.
- Christendom was a civilization decisively shaped by the story, language, symbols, and rhythms of Christianity.
- Christendom was a political arrangement in which church and state provided mutual, if often uneasy, support and legitimation.
- Christendom was an ideology, a mindset, a way of thinking about God's activity in the world.[3]

In contrast, post-Christendom 'is the culture that emerges as the Christian faith loses coherence within a society that has been definitively shaped by the Christian story and as the institutions that have been developed to express Christian convictions decline in influence'.[4] In this post-Christendom era, the Christian story is no longer central to society but has become marginal, Christians are a minority not the majority, are no longer privileged, and no longer have a dominating influence or control of society and its mores.[5]

The Christendom mindset/culture has shaped our ways of thinking and behaving, personally and in our various systems and structures. Despite the demise of Christendom as a political domain, Christendom's ways of thinking and behaving persist. As Stanley Hauerwas has said, 'Constantinianism is a hard habit to break.'[6]

As the church adjusts from a position of central influence to peripheral relevance in society, what might this renegotiated way of being in the world mean for relationships between women and men, which throughout Christendom have been dominated by a hierarchically ordered gender pattern? As the inherent power and privilege of Christendom is unmasked, deconstructed and rejected, what is to be put in its place and what might this mean for women and men?

A Word About Order

Order was important in ancient Greece. The emerging Greek city-state, the *polis*, was governed by the consent of the people through elected representatives and the rule of law. These arrangements, which replaced autocratic rule by a monarch or ruling elite, required observable and measurable standards by which society would conduct its affairs. Rooted in the Hellenistic concern 'for mathematically based precision in various fields of human relations',the democratic rhetoric of the *polis* made frequent reference to 'the carpenter's rule or canon . . . as a metaphor for accuracy, definiteness, and truth'.[7] A stable society was a well-ordered one, with clear and exact regulation. The people who participated in the *polis* were, of course, all free males; women, slaves and those not born in the particular *polis* were excluded.

The early church adopted much of the form of the Greek *polis*: its people's assembly, the *ekklesia*, was governed by an elected council with an elected or appointed overseer. This had implications for the way the early Christians conducted themselves for 'lurking in the word *ekklesia* is the idea that the faithful have a collective responsibility for decisions about the future of the *polis*, just as the people of a *polis* did in ancient Greece'.[8] As we shall see in Chapter 2, the tensions that emerged among early Christian households as a result of women's and men's, both slave and free, Spirit-infused participation in their assemblies had to be negotiated in the midst of the ordered social organization of the Greco-Roman world that was so vital for the preservation of name, family, land, inheritance and state.

The idea of order was important also in Christendom. It was an interpretive framework for looking at life. David Dungan has explored how the metaphor of canon, while appearing frequently in the first three centuries in reference to the apostolic tradition and teaching of the churches (although not to biblical texts), only became used in the sense of law and of a canon of Scripture in the fourth century with Constantine's intervention in church organization.[9] This hermeneutics of order (see further below) that characterized Christendom included a gender hierarchy. Even our language reflects Christendom's ordering of social relations; the phrase 'men and women' comes more naturally to us than 'women and men', which someone commented felt as odd as saying 'Wise and Morecambe'.[10] This book is dis-ordering gender relationships in its title. The disorder I am proposing is not about advocating chaos but of dismantling the Christendom system of male dominance and female subordination.

Patriarchy

The gender hierarchy that characterizes relationships between women and men is something most likely associated with patriarchy rather than with Christendom. Indeed, patriarchy predates Christendom. So what is the relationship between the two?

Patriarchy can be a difficult term for some Christians, given the prominence and esteem with which biblical patriarchs are held. Patriarchy is where the rule of the father is the basic principle of social organization of the family and of society as a whole (which, of course, is very much the story of the biblical patriarchs). Patriarchy has shaped both social systems and the cultural symbols about the nature of reality (that is, theology), into 'a hierarchy of male over female, father over sons, master over slaves (servants)'.[11] So it is not only about the power of men over women, but is also a system of power which shapes society at all levels. It does not exclude the attitudes and actions of individuals, but nor is it limited to that. Patriarchy is a useful concept because it does not apportion blame to men because they are men, but rather names a system that variously rewards men within it and women who co-operate or survive in it, and it is a system that is hostile to any who work to change it.

Clearly, there are links between patriarchal and Christendom models of social organization. But this is not only because of the similar pattern of dominance and subordination evident in each. These links are not merely similar patterns, but mutually reinforcing and interconnected structures of dominations. Given that women and men are also located in diverse social contexts based on numerous factors such as ethnicity, class and nationality, Elisabeth Schüssler Fiorenza has coined the terms kyriarchy and kyriocentrism (derived from the Greek *kyrios*) to mean domination by the emperor, lord, master, father, husband, elite propertied male and thereby to 'express the intersecting structures of dominations' within the ethos of empire. She argues that women's oppression is not only one aspect of this ethos but 'crucial to the maintenance of kyriarchal or imperial cultures and religions'.[12]

As women and men we are in an interconnected web of social relations. Our awareness of one or more particular aspects of our social location may depend on our circumstances at any given time. On the other hand, the complexity of the social systems we are part of may prevent us from being able to see the various dynamics at work in our lives. In this book I focus on the social relations of women and men after Christendom, examining the impact of, and exploring alternative possibilities to, Christendom's shaping of gender relations, of the relationship between the sexes.

Sex and Gender

Sex and gender are terms that tend to be used loosely and fluidly. We often assume we are all talking about the same thing in the way we use them, but we may not be. Sometimes the meaning of the two is conflated and at other times given distinct understandings. Sex and gender are part of the language we employ to talk about humanity as female and male and our varying usage reflects the various debates and ways of thinking about ourselves as women and men.

The word gender is now used synonymously with the word sex and, arguably, is replacing it. While the 2011 UK Census of Population asked whether our sex is female or male, many British (application, monitoring and information) forms use the language of gender to ask if we are female or male. In part, this preference for the term gender may reflect how the term sex has become associated in general usage with sex-acts rather than a biological distinction and the use of gender avoids the ambiguity (and perhaps the embarrassment) that using the term sex might involve.

The previous distinction usually made between sex and gender was of sex as the biological category of being female or male and gender as the expected attributes and behaviours of girls and boys, of women and men. Gender speaks of the way any given society believes biologically differentiated women and men ought to be and should behave, that is, what is properly feminine and masculine. So sex is about the fact of sexual differentiation and gender is about the meaning we give to this sexual distinction.

Debates abound as to whether gender, understood distinctly from sex, is biologically determined (an essentialist view) or culturally conditioned (a constructionist view), or a mixture of both. In other words, does the fact that women are female automatically mean that women are more suited to the care and nurture of others and are good at emotional housework,[13] while because men are male they are more suited to leadership roles, the competition of the marketplace, and rational decision-making? Do men need a warrior God they can relate to, while women respond to a God with a loving father's heart? As unsophisticated (although not necessarily exaggerated) as these stereotypes are, the dichotomy they represent undergirds much recent and contemporary discussion both within and outside of the church about Christian communities and wider society.

In contrast to the essentialist idea that gendered behaviour is biologically determined, a constructionist view sees gender as a product of social and cultural, including religious, influences. While we may not be entirely free of such forces, for we cannot escape to some neutral environment, we may nevertheless choose to challenge the symbols and practices that perpetuate injustice in gender relations and encourage different nurturing environments that do not do so. For it is the injustice in the way that gender is constructed that is the concern. Gender has largely been conceived of in oppositional binary terms: men are strong, women are weak; men are rational, women are emotional; men are leaders, women are followers; men are more suited to the public world of work, business and politics, women to the private world of domesticity, children and care. Not only have women been restricted in their participation in so-called masculine enterprises, but in the gender hierarchy, so-called feminine tasks have been valued less (and paid less) than their opposite male counterpart. For the sex–gender system (that sees gendered roles linked to biological sex) is a value system that places the things associated with maleness of higher worth than those to do with women, as is illustrated, for example, by the status of care and carers in society. As Mary Stewart Van Leeuwen points out, despite cultural diversity in the way tasks are allocated on the basis of sex, 'What is universal is the higher status of whatever is considered "men's work." If in one culture it is men who build houses and women who make baskets, then that culture will see house building as more important than basket-weaving. In another culture, perhaps next door, where women construct houses and men make baskets, basket-weaving will have higher social status than house-building.'[14]

The distinction between sex and gender is enormously helpful in highlighting how culture shapes the significance we give to our biological distinction. For example, biological differences in regard to men generally having greater physical strength and women's child-bearing capacity 'acquire differing values only within the framework of human culture'.[15] In other words, the fact of these differences cannot account for the tendency in human culture to give higher esteem to those with greater physical strength rather than those who bear children. This allows us to ask difficult questions of our social organization and look at things we take for granted.

At the same time, however, we are not disembodied beings. Nor do we form our identities in a 'neutral' human form. Our cultural human experience is mediated only through our female or male (or indeed transgender[16] or intersex) bodies just as our embodied experience is mediated through our various cultural environments. As Elaine Graham has said, 'bodies are neither irrelevant nor all-determining'.[17] A gendered human experience is unavoidable, but it is not static or unchanging. 'A view of human personhood as gendered, therefore, understands it as a process of entering and inhabiting a gendered culture; as simultaneously being the creators, and creatures, of gender relations. Such a gendered culture is forged from the practices and conventions of science, work, technology, religion, reproduction and child-rearing, work, sexuality, power, symbolic exchange and language.'[18]

The dis-order of gender relationships in this book is not about denying gender, but about re-thinking and re-forming our understanding and practice away from a hierarchy of power and binary opposites on the basis of sex.

Sexuality

Sexuality is part of our embodiment as corporeal beings. Our sexuality may be expressed appropriately in numerous ways depending on a variety of contexts, and should not be reduced only to sex-acts or reproductive function. This book is not about romantic or sexual relationships, although there are implications for both in exploring the lives of women and men (not least in rejecting the sexual objectification of anyone as to do so is to violate their personhood). It does, however, concern sexuality in its broadest sense – that as female and male we are sexual beings.

Sexuality is another dimension of human relationships in systems of domination and subordination. The story of women and men within Christendom is not only one of a gender hierarchy, but also one of a normative heterosexuality. In other words, it is about the regulation of the lives of women and men whom it assumes are heterosexual. This heterosexual gender order excludes and makes illegitimate differing – lesbian, gay, bisexual and transgender (LGBT)[19] – sexualities.

While this book is not concerned with romantic or sexual relationships, the fact of our sexuality does pose a question. Does writing about women and men without giving attention to differing sexualities mean ignoring aspects of being female or male for LGBT people in a way that leaves part of the domination/subordination system in place? Put another way, is writing about women and men without reference to their sexual identity to privilege heterosexuality over differing sexualities?

Sexuality (including its orientation) is part of our identity as people – it is part of who we are. The extent to which our sexuality monopolizes our self-understanding and other people's perceptions of us will vary depending on the wider contexts in which we live. So, for many people who are heterosexual, for much of the time, their orientation is the assumed norm in society, from which people who are not heterosexual are viewed as different. While the sexual behaviour of people who are heterosexual may come under scrutiny, not only among churches but in society more generally, lesbian women and gay men are more likely to experience not only their behaviour but their identity, that is, their sense of themselves, being questioned and evaluated. A 'neutral' stance on women and men therefore is arguably one that operates on heterosexist assumptions and norms, which in effect are hidden from view, while at the same time ignoring the lived experience and understanding of LGBT people.

Differing sexualities do raise questions for gender relations because they unsettle norms of being and behaviour for women and men. At the same time, all women and men, regardless of their sexuality, are subject to the expectations and judgements concerning gender relations as they have been manifest within Christendom, which has assumed heterosexuality. My approach in this book is based on the belief that liberating ourselves from the oppressive elements of Christendom's (heterosexual) gender hierarchy is good news for all of us, regardless of how we understand our sexual identity.

Hermeneutics

Finally, a comment on hermeneutics, a term which I use in a broad and also a more particular sense in this book. Hermes was the Greek name for the divine messenger of the gods and patron of eloquence. From his name is derived the Greek verb meaning 'interpret' from which we take the term hermeneutics, which is concerned with the theory – or science and art – of interpretation.

While we are perhaps more used to applying theories of interpretation to the Bible, hermeneutics is about how we interpret or understand not only written texts, 'but the interpretation and understanding of any act of communication, whether written or oral, verbal or non-verbal (such as symbols or symbolic acts)'.[20] It is about how we give meaning to our reality. A hermeneutics of order[21] (mentioned above), therefore, is one that frames social and indeed national relationships within particular Christendom hierarchies, including that of gender. In contrast, Stuart Murray refers to a post-Christendom vision for political order informed by a 'hermeneutic of justice, rather than order, that prioritises the powerless and poor'.[22] So, a hermeneutics of justice would not be oriented toward maintaining a social and political order designed to sustain a Christian empire, but rather be focused on equitable, fair and just treatment for those in society without power and wellbeing.

The use of the term hermeneutics in this book refers to frameworks for understanding gender relations. So Chapter 4 examines the idea of equality as a more just hermeneutics – as a more
even-handed way of structuring relationships between women
and men. Chapter 7 suggests the notion of friendship as a paradigm for gender relationships, inviting us to imagine ourselves
differently. A hermeneutics of friendship is one that envisages us
situated side by side, not men above women. Hermeneutics in its
wider sense is about the interpretative lenses we use to see and
shape our world.[23]

In a more specific sense, biblical hermeneutics deals with
how we interpret the Bible. This, too, is a concern in this book.
Involved in any biblical hermeneutics is discerning how our own
cultural context informs how we read the text. So we not only
have to learn about the first-century world in order to get the
significance of New Testament narratives. (For if we do not know
about the long-standing hostility between Jews and Samaritans,
we fail to comprehend the point of the parable of the good Samaritan.)[24] We also have to think about the influence of our own time
and place upon our grasp of the biblical meaning. (Hence, we are
overly familiar with the parable of the good Samaritan, so much
so that we empathize and identify with the Samaritan. We are not
surprised that it was he who responded to the person in need,
and there is no shock value for us in this parable; it has ceased, in
effect, to function as a parable for us in the way it would have for
its first hearers.)

Often we are more comfortable with the idea of crossing the
historical distance between ourselves and the text than we are
with the idea that we must examine our own situations. This is
particularly acute in considering gender relations. Centuries of
dominant (Christendom) tradition have informed us that the text
espouses a male/female hierarchy and so we find it hard to see it
any other way. Part of the aim of this book is to show it is possible to
have different encounters with the text, thereby inviting different
encounters between contemporary women and men.

2.

Women and Men Before Christendom

If we are to identify the impact of Christendom on the relationship between women and men, we must first have some picture
of what the situation was before Christianity became the religion
of the empire. But which situation? Almost three centuries and
several generations of Christians had passed from the time Jesus
had begun proclaiming the good news. These were the nearly
three hundred years that had seen the growth of both the Roman
Empire and the Christian church and much conflict between the
two. This chapter traces the shape of gender relationships during
this time.

The dominant pattern for relationships between women and
men was patriarchy, which regulated the behaviour of both in
ways that meant men controlled much of women's lives. Patriarchy, of course, predates not only Constantine's imperial rule
but also the Christian church. It is a highly adaptive system that
can mould and meld with many religious and political contexts,
sharing commonalities with other hierarchical systems. As we
shall see, patriarchy was so entangled with the structures of the
Roman Empire that challenging the former was to threaten the
latter.

Setting the Scene

Constantine's adoption of Christianity in 312, which inaugurated
the Christendom era, came in the middle of four centuries of evolu-
tion and change for the church. 'Between the years AD 100 and AD
500 the Christian church changed almost beyond recognition',

writes Tony Lane.[1] From being a small minority faith, spasmod-
ically persecuted, Christianity became the official religion of the
Roman Empire. Rather than individual gospels and epistles circulating among the churches, a canon of Scriptures containing the
Old and New Testaments was established. Instead of the briefest
of early church affirmations such as 'Jesus is Lord', and varied
forms of worship, there were two formal creeds widely used as
part of fixed liturgical worship and as tests of orthodoxy. And the
way churches organized had gone from being fluid and region-
ally varied to a fixed threefold pattern of bishops, presbyters and
deacons.[2]

The intervention of Constantine was instrumental in creating
or consolidating much of this change. His choosing not simply to
tolerate but to increasingly favour Christianity as the religion of
the empire ended the persecution of Christians and set a precedent that nearly all subsequent emperors followed. (By the end
of the fourth century there were imperial decrees making Christianity the only legitimate imperial religion and banning those who
were not Christians from service in the army, the imperial administration or at court. Then in 529 the Byzantine emperor and legal
reformer, Justinian, issued an edict making conversion to Christianity compulsory.) It was Constantine, just a year on from his legitimization of Christianity, who set in motion church councils. Faced
with church disagreement over the appointment of the bishop in
Carthage, Africa (whose followers became known as Donatists),
Constantine decided not to use the imperial legal system to make a
judgement to resolve this dispute. Rather, he called a church council
of bishops from across the Mediterranean to settle the matter and
thereby arrive at a unified church that he believed so important for
the continued favour of the Christian God on his empire. While
this council in Rome in 313 did not achieve its aim (and neither
did the council in Arles which he convened the following year in
a further attempt to bring the dispute to a harmonious conclu-
sion), emperor-convened councils became an established pattern
in the fourth century. The Council of Constantinople, called by
the Eastern Emperor Theodosius in 381, resulted in what is today
known as the Nicene Creed. These councils, attended by bishops
from throughout the Roman Empire, sought to determine issues of
orthodox authority, belief and practice.

However, the pattern of church leadership to which Constantine related – that of bishops, at first of a city and then increasingly of an area – had been established long before he was born. From numerous ecclesial struggles out of concerns for preserving tradition, matters of religious truth, ensuring appropriate discipline and an overall unified church, throughout the many places where Christianity had spread, one dominant pattern emerged. This was of one universal church led by those with a God-given line of authority from apostles.

The oldest known written account of the idea of apostolic succession appears in the writing of Clement – a church leader in Rome – at the end of the first century.[3] In the early part of the second century, from Ignatius, Bishop of Antioch, we have the earliest known written use of the Greek term for general, whole or universal from which we derive 'catholic', used of the one church. It was Ignatius who argued for an episcopal ministry in which one person was the focus for the church who could resist wrong belief and preside over the Eucharist and baptisms.[4]

By the end of the third century, although not without challenge, the pattern of a threefold ministry of deacon, priest and bishop was the assumed norm for the universal church, with greater prominence attached to the bishops in the cities of Antioch and Alexandria in the East and Rome in the West.[5] While also not without challenge and with some exceptions, this leadership was predominantly male but not necessarily celibate. This contrasts with the more fluid organization of the first churches, which used the terms elders and overseers more loosely along with apostles, prophets and teachers, and in which church leadership and role was based on charismata – appropriating gifting from God that was bestowed on both women and men.

So, how did this come about? To understand this we first need to look at the social order of the Greco-Roman world in which the church emerged.

Social Order of the Greco-Roman World

Talk of families and social order, and the place of women and men within this, is very much part of our contemporary political discourse. Arguments abound over what kind of families make for a stable society. Our terminology is varied: two-parent and lone-parent families, single mothers and absent fathers, working and staying-at-home mothers, carers and breadwinners, married and cohabiting couples, marriages and civil partnerships. Yet for all the diversity and often heated debate that this language represents, it is all far away from the familial and social patterns of the time into which Jesus and then the first churches were born.

Relationships between women and men in the Greco-Roman world at the time of Jesus were set in the dual contexts of the *familia* and the *domus*. While our word 'family' is derived from the Latin word *familia*, contemporary families (of whatever kind) are not the modern-day equivalent of the Greco-Roman *familia*. The *familia* referred not to a group of people related by blood, marriage or consenting partnership, but to a household or estate, 'a residential unit for production, consumption and service',[6] that encompassed not only people – including slaves and their children, and ex-slaves who stilled owed service, blood relatives and adopted children – but also property, land and animals. All these people and things were legally under the sovereign control of the *paterfamilias*, the male head of the household. The exception would be offspring (both females and males) who had been emancipated by their father during his lifetime and hence had control over their own property (with daughters subject to certain legal restrictions on their autonomy through male guardianship).[7] In the most common form of marriage, a wife remained under the authority of her own father rather than that of her husband. This had the effect of keeping her dowry property under the domain of her father on divorce (or with herself, subject to male guardianship, if she was married at the time of her father's death) and not left with her former husband.[8]

The strictly understood *familia* norms related to the *domus* or house, which referred to kinship networks of the male lineage of blood descendants through the generations. These two frameworks worked together in the task of 'maintaining and reproducing the male lineage with all its rights of power and property'.[9] The importance of generational family continuity is reflected in the use of adoption to legally secure the transmission of family property and name often in the absence of, and sometimes after disinheriting, a biological heir. This latter, which occurred when a daughter or son had brought shame or disrepute to the family, required public justification 'demonstrating the extent to which family life was not a private matter as it is in our time'.[10] The adoption process, which required seven witnesses, brought the adopted son onto the same legal standing as any biological child.[11] This is the context on which Paul draws to illustrate how believers, through adoption, become children, and hence heirs, of God.[12]

Jewish households reflected a similar patriarchal pattern. Inheritance was passed to sons and daughters (though not necessarily equally to all children), marriages involved dowries, and fathers might gift their daughters other wealth so as to keep it within their own family rather than that of the husband whether or not divorce ensued. While only Roman citizens could enter into marriages covered by Roman law (making them licit marriages), the same cultural expectations about family obligations and honour infused many informal (illicit) marriages in the Greco-Roman world. For some Jews, in contrast to the Roman interest in marriages based on status, there was a concern for marrying within the kin group such as cousins, and perhaps also the practice of polygamy.[13]

Given the diversity contained within kin-households, the lived experience of women and men depended on which women and men we are talking about. Slavery was widespread in the ancient world. Greeks and Jews were both slave owners and slaves.[14] Even relatively poor families might own one or two slaves. The lives of slave women and men were different from that of free-born women and men, who may or may not have been part of the elite in Roman society. As Lynn Cohick succinctly puts it, in the Greco-Roman world, 'Gender is often trumped by status.'[15] Those slave, freed or free-born men who were poor would have had very different fortunes to those of an emancipated, wealthy woman of high status, who might have important responsibilities running a household and even some legal autonomy. There could be a variety of fortunes among slaves themselves, from those who were able to gain skills and favour and perhaps earn their freedom, to those who could be sold on by their masters, separated from their partners and/or children. Female slaves generally had lower skills than male slaves so their earning power and opportunities were reduced and, for many slave women, prostitution for the profit of their owner was a seamless part of their slave experience.

The dominant cultural value of this hierarchical and gendered patriarchal framework of the 'kin-household'[16] was so pervasive that Jesus used its familiarity easily in his parables.[17] There are stories involving masters, sons, slaves and hired workers in settings of household economies and kin relationships. The opportunities and misfortunes of the characters in these stories were well known in actual lives. To be entrusted with responsibilities of wealth generation for a master might fall to a slave (Matt. 25:14), but their failure to succeed could lead to disaster (Matt. 25:30). Indeed, to be sold on, along with your wife, children and possessions, at the decision of a master was unremarkable (Matt. 18:25). However, as with so much of Jesus' teaching, the illustrations he used some-times were effective because of the contrast to prevailing practice, as in the extraordinary notion that a master, on coming home and finding his slaves alert and waiting for him, would have them sit down and he serve them himself (Luke 12:35–8).

The kin-household framework, as with Jewish households, was the primary place of religious identity and observance. In Greco-Roman society, religious identity was not primarily individual or personal but familial. To be a member of a particular kin-house-hold was to have the religious identity of the *paterfamilias*: 'It was generally accepted, as a matter of good civil order, that slaves as well as wives practice the religion of their masters or husbands and preserve the religious ancestral customs of the house.'[18] Reli-gion was integral to the welfare of both kin-households and the state, the patriarchal family being a paradigm for the state. 'As official Roman religion effected a symbiotic relationship between Rome and her gods, whereby the well-being of both was mutually intertwined, so, too the well-being of the Roman *familia* was inex-tricably bound up with the proper veneration of the household gods.'[19] Religion was closely connected with the reproduction of both lineage and national identity. The proper order of the house-hold was reflected in the proper order of the state, and both were cemented in a religiously ordered world. For:

in late antiquity, practically no one doubted that there was a sacral order to the world, or that the social, the political, the cosmic, and the religious realms of human existence were always inextricably involved with one another. Every state was also a cult, or a plurality of cults; society was a religious dispensation; the celestial and political orders belonged to a single continuum; and one's allegiance to one's gods was also one's loyalty to one's nation, people, masters, and monarchs.[20]

Within a generation of Jesus' death,[21] to be a Christian (whether Jewish or Gentile) was to be part of a proscribed *superstitio*, that is, an illicit religion, 'denoting an intolerable deviation from society's norms of behavior'.[22] Some 150 years later, Christians were still accused of being 'a gang . . . of discredited and proscribed desperadoes who band themselves against the gods'[23] with all the implications about disloyalty to household and state. The reasons behind such censure are found in the gospel itself.

Foes in the Household

Greco-Roman kin-households existed (as did Jewish families) to preserve lineages, civic wellbeing, and religious and national identities. Against this background, it is possible to see the enormous threat that Christian allegiance was to the stability of family networks and hence to social order. Where there was household conversion (as happened in Philippi with the Gentile, God-fearing businesswoman, Lydia, and Paul and Silas' Roman jail keeper, and in Corinth with Crispus, a Jewish synagogue official[24]) the entire household followed the decision of the head of the household although this could threaten the larger kin network. But for individuals within households to move away from the religion of the house was to disrupt the conditions for the wellbeing of family and state and threaten the preservation of national identity. This explains the conflict that Jesus talked about for his followers between family members: 'For I have come to set a man against his father, and a daughter against her mother, and a daughter-in-law against her mother-in-law; and one's foes will be members of one's own household' (Matt. 10:35f.).

So what do the gospels tell us about how disruptive, even subversive, to this patriarchal pattern of family and state following Christ could be?

Jesus preached good news of God's liberation in people's lives whereby they are brought into a new community – a kin network that did not depend on blood lines, national identity, or patriarchal norms. Jesus identifies his followers as his family members: 'Whoever does the will of God is my brother and sister and mother' (Mark 3:35). This new community is for everyone, not just Jews. Jesus commends the faith of a Gentile centurion: 'I tell you, not even in Israel have I found such faith' (Luke 7:9); a Canaanite woman: 'Woman, great is your faith!' (Matt. 15:28); and a Samaritan man: 'Your faith has made you well' (Luke 17:19). The message of the Lord's favour that releases the captives and frees the oppressed, announced in Galilee (Luke 4:18), is to be proclaimed to all the nations (Luke 24:47). It is for women as well as men: 'Mary has chosen the better part, which will not be taken away from her' (Luke 10:42). It is for children as well as adults: 'Let the little children come to me; do not stop them: for it is to such as these that the kingdom of God belongs' (Mark 10:14). Further, it includes those of low status and without rights on the same basis and even on occasions instead of those of wealth and status. In a parable of a great dinner to which the invited guests made excuses not to attend, their places were taken by 'the poor, the crippled, the blind, and the lame' (Luke 14:21). This good news radically transforms the behaviour of the powerful. In response to the anger of the other disciples on discovering the request of James and John to sit on either side of Jesus 'in your glory', Jesus said:

> You know that among the Gentiles those whom they recognize as their rulers lord it over them, and their great ones are tyrants over them. But it is not so among you; but whoever wishes to become great among you must be your servant, and whoever wishes to be first among you must be slave of all. For the Son of Man came not to be served but to serve, and to give his life a ransom for many. (Mark 10:42-5)

This good news was deeply subversive of the prevailing social order and was the outworking of the picture of God presented by Jesus. In the gospels, Jesus presents God as 'father' – his own and of those who follow him. Much thinking about the significance of God as father today focuses on what we might know of God from our experience of human fathers and what we can learn about how human fathers ought to behave given that God is depicted in this way. Within this focus, both implicitly and explicitly, much is made of father as *a male and not a female* depiction of God and the import of that for our ideas about God and about human relationships.[25] These are matters of much contemporary debate that rests on gender identity as the lens through which God as father is to be understood.

There is, however, another way of reading the depiction of God as father, that it is a metaphor used not for its value as male as opposed to female imagery, but as a juxtaposition to 'king' or 'master'. What Jesus is conveying is that God is not like an earthly king who rules over subservient subjects but a father who cares for his children. The idea of God as father draws on a familial term of belonging rather than a term of allegiance to a master or king. It is relationship to this father that makes one a member of God's family – it is not dependent on biological lineages or existing religious loyalties (whether Jewish or pagan).

The idea of belonging based on relationship to the father of the family would have made sense against the background of both Greco-Roman and Jewish households. But in contrast to the power of the *paterfamilias*, there are no slaves – people are not owned like property – there are only brothers and sisters and friends.[26] There is no competition for status and power, for self-promotion, or jostling for positions of greatness.[27] Nor is the accumulation of wealth a priority, indeed it is a hindrance.[28] And existing family loyalties are superseded.[29] This is a picture of God that undermines, challenges and opposes the hierarchy of patriarchal families – of whatever kind.

Deirdre Good demonstrates how this challenge is presented in the Gospel of Matthew, written for Christians from a Jewish community.[30] Against the reality of Jewish traditions of family and inheritance, in which genealogy – blood ties – were determinative not only of *who* was included but also of who *could* be included in the community, Matthew presents God as the only legitimate father. In contrast to the accepted place of a human father as the authority in a family, Matthew places God the Father as the source of authority for the community of Christian believers. So thorough is this treatment in the gospel, nowhere does Matthew use the

term father to describe human beings (other than as an identifier
between two people of the same name) and records Jesus saying,
'Call no one your father on earth, for you have one Father – the
one in heaven.'[31] While kinship in Jewish families was determined
by biology and blood, in the new Christian community, family
membership is based on behaviour – those who do the will of the
Father in showing compassion to those in need. What is more, this
behaviour may be deliberately or unintentionally in accord with
the will of the Father, and those who demonstrate their belonging
to the new family in this way will inherit all that is due to family
members – the kingdom of heaven.[32]

What our own cultural discourse about family can prevent us
from seeing is that God as father is not used as 'a legitimization
for existing patriarchal structures in society or church but as a
critical subversion of all structures of domination'.[33] God's new
family framework was highly subversive of the existing social and
indeed political order. According to Celsus, a pagan critic of Christianity, writing toward the end of the second century, Christians
of lower classes were guilty of persuading children and women
to defy the authority of fathers and tutors and to become Christians. These lowly Christians were 'wool-workers, cobblers, and
laundry workers, and the most illiterate and bucolic yokels' who
'get hold of children . . . and some stupid women' and make 'some
astounding statements as, for example, they must not pay any
attention to their father and schoolteachers, but must obey them;
they say that these talk nonsense and have no understanding . . .
they alone know the right way to live.'[34] What this unsympathetic
and indeed hostile partial portrait shows is that for Celsus, Christianity – a religion of women, children and slaves – threatened the
cohesion of the *familia*, and therefore the wellbeing of the empire.

Living in the End Days

This dis-orderly family behaviour was further compounded by
the eschatological expectations of the first Christians. Many of the
first Christians believed that Christ had inaugurated a new age that
would be realized sooner rather than later, even in their own lifetime.
They were living in the last days[35] and anticipated Jesus returning.[36]

This expectation shed fresh light on their everyday lives. The things of this world were to pass away, and a new kingdom begin. One response to this common eschatological expectation was not to take part in the social convention of kin and household through neither marrying nor remarrying or through sexual renunciation within marriage. After all, if inclusion in the kingdom of God was not dependent on belonging to the nation of Israel or following the pagan gods of Greco-Roman households, but came rather through belonging to a new family in God, then maintaining conventional households and family lineages was no longer necessary. This was one of the crucial issues for the socially diverse (rich and poor, masters and slaves, women and men), majority Gentile Christians at Corinth fresh in their experience of extraordinary Spirit-filled behaviour who were seeking to live lives appropriate to this new age.

Prompted by the Corinthian Christians' inclination to be sexually abstemious – 'Now concerning the matters about which you wrote: "It is well for a man not to touch a woman"' (1 Cor. 7:1) – Paul wrote to them indicating appropriate behaviour for those who were married (about remaining married or not and about sex within marriage) and those who were not married or widowed (about remaining so unless unable to be sexually chaste).[37] Opinions differ as to Paul's overall stance about these matters. Is he presenting radical challenges to household patterns or in fact furthering social conformity and hence respectability? While he presents a remarkable equal mutuality of wives and husbands in terms of their sexual relations,[38] and in terms of marriage as a choice for both women and men to challenge sexual passion if they cannot be self-controlled,[39] he also seems particularly concerned about male self-control.[40] While on the one hand he discourages marriage because of the attention it requires and the anxieties it generates[41] and indeed favours celibacy over marriage and sex,[42] he warns against divorce[43] and appears to leave other household structures in place, encouraging slaves to remain in their servitude.[44]

What sense are we to make of these apparent contradictions? Paul's consistent concern in his instructions – 'my rule in all the churches' (1 Cor. 7:17) – is that the Christians should remain as they were,[45] due to the impending crisis,[46] for 'the appointed time has grown short' (1 Cor. 7:29) and the usual way of things would no longer apply[47] as 'the present form of this world is passing away' (1 Cor. 7:31). This in itself shows a lack of interest in perpetuating the normal concerns of households. But further than this, Paul's affirmation of remaining unmarried is extraordinary for 'in the first century, permanent abstinence from sexual relations and remaining unmarried were quite exceptional'.[48] The Jewish ascetic communities that we know of from this period (the Essene community at Qumran and the Therapeutae near Alexandria) were isolated from mainstream urban society. Marrying and child-bearing were integral to women's lives in Roman society, the birth rate and number of children a matter of political concern. The emperor Augustus (who was reigning when Jesus was born) introduced severe marriage legislation including sanctions and taxes upon those who were still bachelors, and there was an expectation that widowers, widows and divorcees would remarry, with only those over fifty or sixty years of age allowed to remain unmarried. While this 'flurry of legal activity criminalizing immorality and promoting marriage'[49] may not have been enforced or indeed enforceable throughout the empire, it clearly indicates a dominant cultural and legal ethos that did not support remaining unmarried.[50]

In this context, Paul's admonishment to the Christians at the urban centre of Corinth to remain unmarried (either for the first or subsequent times) is striking. This renunciation of marriage was inextricably linked to a rejection of the economic, civic and political patterns of the day. The fabric of society depended on the organization of marriage and household. Non-marriage and sexual abstinence was a 'drastic alternative to the moral and social order that seemed so secure'.[51] It was 'through sex and marriage, "the world" as a social system of power and possessions was reproduced. To renounce marriage was to renounce that "world" in all its social, economic, and political implications.'[52] In the face of the given cultural realities of the dominant status quo, however, such renunciation was hard to sustain.

Living in the World

Christians in the first century were a socially diverse group. There were well-off householders, both women and men, many of whom hosted churches and visiting teachers/prophets in their homes. There were also poorer people and those who needed financial and practical support from other believers. There were both free women and men, and slave women and men, and children. They were single, married, widowed and divorced. They came from Jewish, God-fearing and pagan religious backgrounds. Believers met in households to worship together, to pray and prophesy, to teach and learn, to share a Last Supper meal together, with both women and men participating in these activities. They had internal struggles over their relationships and behaviour as they sought to live out their new life in Christ, a new life that dismantled former boundaries of superiority/inferiority, as expressed in what is considered by many to be an early Christian baptismal confession: 'There is no longer Jew or Greek, there is no longer slave or free, there is no longer male and female; for all of you are one in Christ Jesus' (Gal. 3:28). And they did this in the midst of a society and culture that found their allegiances in this new community threatening to social order and stability.

Many threads from the character(s) of these churches continued into the following two centuries before Constantine. In the second half of the first century, however, with eschatological expectations not met and continuing tensions with the surrounding society, Christians began adapting to their given situation. The overlapping components of this adaption over the next two centuries included: conformity to patriarchal household patterns in the subordination of women to fathers and husbands, and slaves to householders, which came to be adopted as the pattern for the household of God; the change from an itinerant prophetic and apostolic leadership to local leadership; and a strict division between clergy and laity with an increased emphasis on celibacy for clergy.

New Testament evidence of this change is found in a number of epistles in a variety of ways. In the letter to the Colossian Christians, wives, children and slaves are told to be subject to husbands, parents and masters, respectively, with particular emphasis on the obedience and behaviour of slaves.[53] While the dominant party in each pairing (husbands, fathers – not mothers – and masters) are instructed to temper their behaviour in ways that do not abuse their positions of power, these instructions appear to reflect the

voice of the dominant group. In the letter to the Christians in
Ephesus, these same three pairings are present in similar fashion,
with the greater emphasis on married women and men (but again,
not the relationships of women and men in the Christian community).[54] In 1 Peter, slaves and wives, including those not married
to believers, are addressed, along with husbands more briefly.[55] In
this epistle the context for these remarks is clearly elaborated. In
their moral alienation from the world, Christians are aliens and
exiles, metaphors 'drawn from the technical vocabulary of repub-
lican exclusiveness'[56] that indicate a lack of social acceptability as
those who were not Roman citizens, which may well have been
the actual case for many of the Christians listening to the epistle.
As such, for the sake of their witness and despite opposition,
they must conduct themselves honourably among the Gentiles,
accepting the authority of human institutions and honouring the
emperor.[57]

The concern for 'a quiet and peaceable life in all godliness and
dignity' for believers following 'supplications, prayers, inter-
cessions, and thanksgivings' made for 'kings and all who are in
high positions' is also the behind the injunctions in 1 Timothy.[58]
(This is not necessarily the same thing as blunting the gospel challenge to the current social and political status quo. For example,
the deified emperor was seen as the *paterfamilias* of the empire,
and his presence spoken of as a manifestation of God of whom
he was considered to be an apparition. The letter makes the coun-
terclaim that the Christian God is 'father',[59] and that Jesus who
will be made manifest is the only sovereign.[60] This is 'a deliberate
application to God and Christ Jesus of the Hellenistic terminology
that described the emperor.'[61]) It is this epistle that turns attention to specific matters of the corporate life of believers – about
the behaviour of women,[62] the character of bishops/overseers
and (arguably both female and male) deacons,[63] and regulations
regarding widows (eligibility being if they are not less than sixty
years old, probably reflecting Roman legislation).[64] In particular,
the description of the bishop or overseer is that of a good *paterfamilias*, suggesting patriarchal household governance was being
applied to the governance of the household of believers.

This ordering was not an innovation of early Christians but
clearly echoes known domestic or household codes of antiquity

originating with Aristotle and reiterated by others. For Aristotle, the primary parts of the household were 'master and slave, husband and wife, father and children'. He thought that, as by nature and expediency the body governs the soul, so reason and intellect govern the emotions, and it would be harmful for the two parties to be on equal footing or in reverse situation. Rather, 'the male is by nature superior and the female inferior, the male ruler and the female subject. And the same must also necessarily apply in the case of humankind generally; therefore all human beings that differ as widely as the soul does from the body . . . these are by nature slaves for whom to be governed by this kind of authority is advantageous.'[65]

Proper household order was essential for the health of the state. Occasions when women flouted this were frowned upon. The Roman historian Livy recounts the reaction in 195 BC of Roman consul Cato to Roman women protesting in public against the Oppian law.[66] Cato argues that if his fellow citizens had established a husband's right and authority over:

> the mother of his own family, we should have less difficulty with women in general . . . What kind of behaviour is this? Running around in public, blocking streets, and speaking to other women's husbands! Could you not have asked your husband the same thing at home? . . . They want freedom, nay licence (if we are to speak the truth) in all things . . . As soon as they begin to be your equals, they will have become your superiors.[67]

Plutarch, the Greek Platonist philosopher, who was born towards the end of the apostle Paul's life, says the speech of the virtuous woman 'ought to be not for the public, and she ought to be modest and guarded about saying anything in the hearing of outsiders', and that a woman 'ought to do her talking either to her husband or though her husband'. When women 'subordinate themselves to their husbands, they are commended . . . and control ought to be exercised by the man over the woman . . . as the soul controls the body'.[68]

It is clear to see how some passages in New Testament epistles reflect this threefold concern for proper authority of masters, husbands and fathers over slaves, wives and children and, in particular, the instructions concerning the behaviour of women in households and in the community household of believers. However, while they reflect the concern of the ancient world, they do not necessarily mirror its remedy. John Howard Yoder has outlined a number of significant ways in which the injunctions in the New Testament epistles differ from the household codes of antiquity, not least in the astonishing way that the former address the persons in subordinate roles as moral agents while the focus of the latter is on the self-actualization of the persons in the positions of dominance.[69] 'Here we have a faith that assigns *personal moral responsibility to those who had no legal or moral status* in their culture, and makes of them decision-makers. It gives them responsibility for viewing their status in society not as a simple meaningless decree of fate but as their own meaningful witness and ministry, as an issue about which they can make a moral choice.'[70] Hence, in contrast to the Stoic emphasis on the person in the dominant role living up to their own nature, the New Testament puts dominant and subordinate pairs in relationship and focuses on the responsibility of each to the other rather than to themselves.[71] What is more, while the resulting behaviour of wives, children and slaves may not be, to outward appearance, very different to what was expected in the social order, for husbands to love their wives, fathers to avoid angering their children, and masters to treat their slaves fairly and justly in the knowledge of the way they have been treated by God would make a concrete and sweeping difference to surrounding social norms. John Howard Yoder describes this call to the dominant partner to a kind of reciprocal subordination a revolutionary trait that undercuts the hierarchical social order.[72]

Interpreting the various household instructions depends, in part, on the authorship of the particular letters. Opinion is divided as to whether they were letters from Paul (in the case of Colossians, Ephesians and Timothy) and Peter or from later followers using the apostles' names for greater authority. If the latter, then it is argued that there was a regression from gospel and apostolic understanding and practice to more socially acceptable norms that were less antagonistic to the surrounding culture in the light of ongoing and indeed increasing tensions.[73] If all the letters are apostolic in authorship, they are often understood as, in the case of Paul, being about becoming 'all things to all people' for the sake of the gospel,[74] with Paul's affirmation that 'there is no longer Jew or Greek, there is no longer slave or free, there is no longer male and female' (Gal. 3:28) being the interpretive lens within which the rest of his writings are to be placed.[75] After all, the household 'admonition is addressed first to persons on the bottom side of the social order, and assumes that they have heard a message which calls into question the subjection they have hitherto not been able to challenge. Where had they heard such a message if not from Paul?'[76]

As I shall return to in Chapter 6, the question of authorship of 1 Timothy has served to obscure the fact that there are other ways of approaching that particular text that offer alternative understanding regardless of its authorship. Whenever written, however, these texts were produced in the same half-century as the gospels (the dating of which is also debated), which, as outlined above, witness to a radical envisioning of human relationships. The New Testament shows us that women (free and slave) received the Spirit, along with (free and slave) men, when it was poured out at Pentecost in prophetic fulfilment of God's ancient promise.[77] These Spirit-filled women were active in their discipleship and in the community life of believers, and this resulted in persecution by Saul of Tarsus who is described as 'ravaging the church by entering house after house; dragging off both men and women' to prison.[78]

It is also the case that the epistle injunctions are given as indicators of what the authors thought ought to be happening, not what the practice and behaviour actually was. In other words, instructions that women restrict their teaching and authority only to women[79] assume that women were involved in teaching and exercising authority in regard to men as well (as the New Testament shows us happened in the case of Priscilla, one of Paul's fellow workers well-known by Gentile churches, who taught Apollos).[80] Indeed, the rhetorical nature of these texts suggests a way of approaching them. As Elisabeth Schüssler Fiorenza has shown, rather than viewing Paul's letters as the voice of a single author (or authors claiming one voice) and attempting to discern whether that voice was pro or anti (various) hierarchies in households and believing communities, we can see them as witnessing to multiple voices and experiences within early Christian groups who were debating how to live out the gospel of Jesus.[81] Recovering these various voices not only helps in understanding the lives of the first generations of Christians, but crucially engages contemporary Christians in similar conversations. 'To read Paul's letter as taking part in such a debate opens up the possibility to reconstruct it in such a way that acknowledges that communities today are still participating in it.'[82]

Diverse Witness

That other more emancipating traditions and practices are inscribed in texts which are prescriptive of women's behaviour is also true of the writings in the immediate centuries after the New Testament period, indicating that some Christians were still seeking to live in accord with their understanding of God's household that overturned patriarchal gender relations. Tertullian, writing at the start of the third century, stated women should be silent in church, not be too bold to learn, let alone teach, and not baptize (even though he asserted that laymen could baptize in the absence of an ordained priest). The early third-century *Didascalia Apostolorum* (Teachings of the Apostles) argues that women were not appointed to teach, preach or to baptize. The late fourth-century *Apostolic Church Order* contains a discussion as to whether or not women can celebrate the Eucharist. The Synod of Laodicea, also fourth century, decreed that women presbytides or women presiders should not be installed in the church and it forbade women to enter the sanctuary. At the end of the fifth century, in a letter to the bishops in southern Italy, Pope Gelasius I complained that women were officiating at the altars in the churches of that region.

Evidence from the New Testament and early church history also indicates a lived understanding of women participating throughout the life of Christian communities. Women were counted among the apostles (a group larger than the twelve disciples gathered by Jesus)[83] in both the New Testament and early churches. For Origen, the Samaritan woman was an apostle and an evangelist, as were, according to Hippolytus of Rome, the women who were the first

witnesses to the resurrection, indicating the missionary compo-
nent of early Christian understanding of apostleship.[84] Junia (or
Julia) is so-named by Paul in Romans 16:7 as someone who was a
believer before he was and who had been imprisoned with him.
Commentaries written on Romans from John Chrysostom in the
fourth century to Peter Abelard in the twelfth, accept Junia/Julia
as a woman; not until Aegidius of Rome (1245–1316) did any
commentator claim the name was masculine and referred to a
man.[85] 'It is significant that Paul, whose letters are a vivid witness
to the conflict over apostolic legitimacy, does not argue on the basis
of gender: according to Paul a genuine apostleship is legitimated
primarily by the commissioning of the Risen One.'[86]

Women participated in the common practice of prophecy in the
early church (1 Cor. 11:4–5). Anna, Elizabeth, Mary (the mother of
Jesus), and the four daughters of Philip from Caesarea are women
named or characterized as prophets.[87] Justin and Irenaeus of Lyons
refer to women as prophets. For Origen, 'women could also share
in the grace of prophecy because this gift is given not according
to the difference of the sexes, but according to the purity of the
mind.'[88] Eusebius acknowledged the second-century prophet
Ammia of Philadelphia.

While in the first two centuries the diaconal office was yet to
formalize, both women and men served as deacons in the early
church. The woman deacon best known to us is the apostle Paul's
co-worker, Phoebe – sister, deacon and benefactor of the church.[89]
Origen cites 'pious Phoebe' as a specific example of the Pauline
apostolic authority for women deacons outlined in 1 Timothy
3:11 and she also appears as a model for women candidates (with
Stephen in this capacity for men) in an extant manuscript from
the tenth century containing ordination rituals for deacons.[90] An
inscription at the Mount of Olives for the deacon Sophia describes
her as a 'second Phoebe'.[91] While Phoebe was most likely a woman
of some prosperity and social standing, two deaconesses imprisoned by Pliny the Younger in 111 were both slave women, itself
an indicator of a counter-culture among the first generations of
Christians.[92] In order to find out more about the church, which
he noted included not only citizens but non-citizens as well as
all classes, age groups and both sexes and was a threat not only
in cities, but also in villages and rural areas, Pliny had these two

women tortured. He was unimpressed with what he learned: 'I found nothing but a depraved and excessive superstition.'[93]

Evidence from the third century on (when church offices became established and settled) reveals how women deacons ministered to women in church gatherings, instructing women catechumens, and performing a large part of baptismal rituals for women:

> they undressed them and anointed their naked bodies with oil like the Roman gladiators, in order to prepare them symbolically for the battle with Satan that they had to survive in baptism in the understanding of the early church. Then they led the women to the pool, submerged them, and clothed them finally with the white garment of the newly baptized. Only the pronouncing of the baptismal formula and the final anointing of the forehead was reserved for the bishop.[94]

In addition, women deacons ministered to women in households, visiting those who were sick, taking them communion, and laying their hands on them in prayer.

Women also served the church through orders of widows. Distinct from widows in need of material and social support because of their circumstances, ecclesiastical widows were women who were active in the church – well attested for good works, hospitable, had washed the feet of the saints, aided the afflicted, and been devoted to doing good in every way.[95] Widows could receive financial support from the church in similar fashion to those in other orders,[96] although not all did because they had independent or family means, such as the Roman widow Regina whose epigraph reads she 'was not a burden to the Church'.[97] Widows received half that which was given to presbyters and deacons, and one quarter of what the bishop received.[98]

In the *Traditio Apostolica* the enrolled widows are listed after the bishops, presbyters, deacons and confessors. While this church order, which was part of the move to restrict sacramental and liturgical service to the clergy,[99] states the widows are chosen and enrolled but not ordained through the laying on of hands, a fifth-century order, *Testamentum Domini*, describes widows as both elected and ordained. It also seats widows next to the bishop at worship. These widows taught women, tested deaconesses, prayed, cared for the sick, and anointed women at baptism.[100]

Enrolled widows were not necessarily only those who had outlived a deceased husband; younger women who had never married and perhaps did not wish to also joined orders of widows. Directions in the *Didascalia* that widows limit their teaching of non-believers to preliminary matters, leaving Christology to be expounded by men so not to have the message scoffed at by Gentiles, show how widows were involved in spreading the gospel to other households.[101] Household life was the focus for much of women's church ministry – 'either women meeting together in a house, seeking to build believing homes, or struggling to preserve Christian allegiance in the home of a pagan householder'.[102]

Rodney Stark has argued that, in contrast to the Roman world in which men outnumbered women, there were greater numbers of women in the church compared to men not only because more women were attracted to Christianity than men, but also because Christians rejected the common pagan practices of infanticide, particularly of female children, and abortion, and because they also affirmed marriage.[103] He contends that their greater number was one reason for their greater participation in the community life of believers, for them having relatively more status and power in Christian subculture than their pagan counterparts.

Christian teaching and instruction among the first generations of Christians was variously carried out by apostles and prophets, presbyters and widows, by bishops and deacons, and by those described as teachers. Following in the footsteps of Priscilla who instructed the well-educated Alexandrian Jewish Christian, Apollos, were Theodora, Macrina, Marcella, and Melania the Younger.[104] In 382, Theodora's husband, Evacrius, inscribed on her tomb that she was 'the best protector of the law and teacher of the faith' who 'throughout her life directed her superior spirit to the saints'.[105] Around the same time, Gregory of Nyssa wrote how he viewed his recently deceased older sister, Macrina, as a theological leader of women and men, lay people and clergy, clearly viewing her as an expert in expounding Scripture. Jerome praised the Christian teacher, Marcella, a Roman woman of wealth and status (who died in 410), for her theological competence and the astute way she taught men, including some male clerics, who came to her for advice, in such a way as to make them comfortable with learning from a woman. Jerome dedicated his commentaries on

Daniel and Galatians to Marcella. The ascetic, Melania the Younger, who founded monasteries in North Africa and Jerusalem, gave instruction to women and men as part of her function as monastic community leader.

Women in the first generations of Christians were benefactors and patrons of believing communities. They participated in worship, prayed and prophesied. They spread the good news and instructed new believers. They participated in church rituals and were among the offices of the increasingly settled ecclesial institution. They were also imprisoned, persecuted and martyred. According to Eusebius, part of Blandina's horrific ordeal in 177 was being hung on a stake in an amphitheatre where 'she seemed to be hanging in the shape of a cross' so that other Christians being beaten and burned 'saw in the form of their sister him who was crucified for them'.[106] In a time when the maleness of Jesus was not called upon as a reason to exclude women from the priesthood,[107] it was perfectly possible for an influential fourth-century churchman to imagine believers being fortified in their faith by a woman embodying the crucified Christ.

While many of women's experiences from these centuries have been overlooked or obscured (and at times denied), they indicate that, despite the increasing dominance of an ordained male episcopal ministry, alternative traditions or practices still existed even as ministry was becoming clericalized.

A Silent Revolution

Peter Brown has described the creation of a strict division between clergy and laity in the Christian church in the second and third centuries as a 'silent revolution'.[108]

With a delay in eschatological expectations of the return of Christ and the growth of Christian communities, many of which were established by the missionary endeavours of apostles and prophets travelling from place to place, it was inevitable that each local group would organize itself in some way. What was not so certain, though, was that this would be based on an episcopal hierarchy of ordained leaders. However, an exclusively male clericalism won out over a more fluid, community-based organic system that relied on the spiritual gifting of many members. Elisabeth Schüssler Fiorenza argues this should not be characterized simply as institutionalization: 'The shift which took place in the second century was not a shift from charismatic leadership to institutional consolidation, but from charismatic and communal authority to an authority vested in local officers, who – in time – absorb not only the teaching authority of the prophet and apostle but also the decision-making power of the community.'[109]

The crucial nature of episcopal authority is seen in the catholic church's conflict with the New Prophecy, which emerged in Phrygia, Asia Minor, in the second half of the second century. A recent convert, Montanus, and then two women, Priscilla and Maximilla, began prophesying the imminent end of the world and advocating appropriate lives of austerity in the light of this, including greater fasting, no fleeing from martyrdom and no marriage. Both Priscilla and Maximilla were criticized for leaving their husbands and embracing a life of celibacy by the church historian Eusebius. The early Montanists (as their opponents called them) had much in common with earlier Christian practice that had relied heavily on prophecy for claims to authority within the Christian community. And they were considered orthodox, even by their opponents, in their acceptance of Old and New Testament Scriptures, and in their view of God as Father, Son and Holy Spirit. Hippolytus of Rome acknowledged that 'they accept all that the gospel testifies about Christ'.[110] Irenaeus (a presbyter, then Bishop of Lyons in Gaul) urged that the movement not be condemned without due consideration (in contrast to his consistent and robust opposition to Gnosticism).

However, the claim to the Spirit as an alternative source of authority from that of the bishops ensured that the New Prophecy was opposed. Perpetua, a Montanist prepared to die rather than renounce her Christian faith against not only the wishes of the ruling state but the pleadings of her own father, epitomized the threat to catholic bishops through her visions. Imprisoned during the persecution under Septimius Severus at the start of the third century, Perpetua saw in a vision her younger brother, Dinocrates, who had died from cancer aged seven before he was baptized, suffering the torments of the unfortunate dead. He was dirty and pale, hot and thirsty and just out of reach of a pool of cool water.

In her captivity, Perpetua prayed for him day and night until she had another vision in which Dinocrates no longer had the fatal cancerous wound on his face, but was clean and refreshed, drinking from the pool of water and happily playing. The implication that it was possible to receive grace without the sacramental role of the episcopal system was deeply antagonistic to the 'bevies of bishops' as Tertullian called them, whom he said did not have the authority to forgive just because they were church officials, this resting rather in spiritual individuals in the church.[111] The matter of forgiveness was a raw concern for Christians in Tertullian's region of North Africa who struggled over whether forgiveness was possible for those who had renounced their faith under persecution. This issue was the catalyst in episcopal election disputes in Carthage and Rome in the mid-third century following a decade of persecution begun by Decius and in the early fourth century in the Donatist controversy over the appointment of a bishop in Carthage in which Constantine became involved. The objection to the spiritual authority claimed by those in the New Prophecy was no small matter.

The challenge and resulting conflict which Montanism posed for the catholic church was exacerbated by women's involvement in the leadership of the movement. As Ross Shepard Kraemer has observed, 'women may not have been prominent in the majority of so-called heresies, but most movements we know to have been characterized by the prominence of women were ultimately judged heretical'.[112] Even one of their own, Tertullian, who became a Montanist after the first generation of the New Prophecy, believed women prophets should exercise a prophetic role within the context of highly restrictive and regulated patriarchal norms for women. The first of the new prophets, however, would not have agreed. Ross Shepard Kraemer considers that what was most interesting about the Montanists was that 'both men and women found compelling a movement in which women were not relegated to the background, but were significant, even central players'.[113]

The transition of authority from the more mobile ministry of prophets and apostles to the settled ministry of presbyters and bishops resulted in submission to episcopal authority becoming a crucial defining characteristic of Christian communities: 'The patristic boundaries no longer established Christian identity over and against its patriarchal society but over and against other Christian social and doctrinal systems.'[114]

It also meant a division between clergy and laity. Lay Christians (including well-off widows) provided material wealth for the church and the maintenance of congregation numbers through bearing children. Wealth was seen as a gift from God that could be bestowed on the church. According to Irenaeus, to accept this view of wealth was to accept the structures of the society that enabled the wealth to be accumulated, which meant viewing the peace of the pagan Roman Empire as one of God's gifts to humanity.[115] Clergy in turn, as a result of their ordination through the laying-on of hands, maintained their exclusive role in the celebration of the Eucharist and protected clerical leadership in the church. They were encouraged to practise perpetual sexual continence even when married, a further sign of their superiority over the laity. Women who also gave themselves to celibate lives eventually became cloistered into privatized monastic enclosures.

Writing early in the fourth century, Eusebius summed up this situation in terms of two ways of life that had been given to the church by Christ:

> The one is above nature, and beyond common human living; it admits not marriage, child-bearing, property nor the possession of wealth . . . Like some celestial beings, these gaze down upon human life, performing the duty of a priesthood to Almighty God for the whole race.

This is 'the perfect form of the Christian life'. In contrast:

> the more humble, more human way prompts men to join in pure nuptials, and to produce children, to undertake government, to give orders to soldiers fighting for right; it allows them to have minds for farming, for trade and for the other more secular interests as well as for religion . . . And a kind of secondary grade of piety is attributed to them.[116]

The outworking of this characterization of two ways would be part of Christianity for centuries to come.

Turning the World Upside Down?

When Paul and Silas spent time in Thessalonica debating with the Jews about Jesus the Messiah, persuading some of them along with 'a great many of the devout Greeks and not a few of the leading women', many Jews objected to their presence and message. A Jewish-provoked mob dragged some new converts before the city authorities protesting that they had entertained as guests those who had been flouting the decrees of the emperor and 'turning the world upside down'.[117]

In the sweep of history, the mini portraits we have of the lives of the first Christians give us only fleeting glimpses of their lived understanding of the extraordinary impact of their new life in Christ, which turned the world upside down. They had a new allegiance to God in Christ which disturbed the alliance between household, state and gods so essential to imperial order and well-being. Their conviction that Christ was the Messiah for the whole world, and their experience of the Spirit that promised the new age was coming, meant their faith endured despite not simply social obstacles but severe opposition and, for some, death for their faith. Being true to this faith and protecting its integrity was vital.

Evolved out of concern to safeguard the unity of the church, by the end of the third century, the threefold hierarchical clerical system of bishop, priest and deacon was established. It embedded a split between clergy and laity, resting authority of leadership, belief and practice in a separated, near exclusively male group of believers. In doing so, it reinforced a belief in a divine ordering of patriarchal gender relationships. While more radical groups persisted, challenging both spiritual and gender hierarchies, they were not considered normative of Christian experience. When Constantine adopted Christianity, bringing to an end a marginal and often persecuted, if not always without wealth and wellbeing, existence for the church, this was the Christianity he encountered and annexed into his empire.

3.

The Gender Order of Christendom

In the eleventh century, a re-energized Catholic Church hierarchy combined with new architectural techniques and began to pierce the skies across Europe with large cathedral churches. Their enormous vaulted ceilings and dominating high towers reached heavenwards, witnessing to divine favour. The light that flooded through their stained-glass windows proclaimed the light of Christian truth to those gathered inside. These new or rebuilt church buildings were testimony to the institutional and devotional renewal in the church: 'each new church was a reform in stone.'[1]

In 1093 building began on one such 'reform in stone' at Durham. Durham Cathedral is set high on a hill with a steep incline to the river winding below. It was finally completed with side chapels and towers in 1280. The greater part of the cathedral was erected in the first half of the twelfth century (by 1133) – that's the nave, which extends from the north door (the entrance to the cathedral) down to the central tower, the north and south transepts, and beyond that an area known as the quire. The quire is the heart of the cathedral, from where, every day since its construction, worship has been offered to God. It is in the quire that the bishop's throne is, which, when built in the latter half of the fourteenth century, was claimed as the highest in Christendom. Beyond the quire is the sanctuary, the cathedral's holiest place, the focal point of which is the high altar.

Back near the north door, in the first section of the nave, there is in the brown stone floor a long, narrow slab of black Frosterley 'marble' (a local stone from Weardale), which is set in the floor and yet is so smoothly blended in that it looks like it is all part of one seamless piece. From the very beginning of the cathedral's existence, this distinctive black stone marked the point beyond which, having entered the cathedral through the north door, women could not go. This was the case for over four hundred years. In 1175 the Galilee Chapel was added to the north end of the cathedral and was the one place in the cathedral that women could worship during these four hundred years. Then at the end of the cathedral's monastic period in the mid-sixteenth century, the black marble restriction ended, and women were able to pass down the nave and into the heart of the cathedral. Not, however, to touch its soul, as the altar was still forbidden to women and would be for a further 450 years until the ordination of women to the priesthood in the Church of England that was realized in 1994. This was not an unqualified access, for male priests and bishops still retained the right not to participate, co-operate or affirm women's priesthood, and individual congregations the right not to have a female priest. Only with such accommodation were women able to enter the priesthood and, at the time of writing, the question of what process is to be put in place, in effect, to continue this accommodation is a matter the Church of England is considering before there is the possibility of a woman sitting in the Cathedra Chair of Durham or any other cathedral in England.[2]

The universal church of Western Christendom, where everyone belonged – indeed where belonging was obligatory – has embedded within it the narrative of the black marble. Christendom's order of hierarchy and dominance was replicated in and mutually reinforced by patriarchal gender relationships. This chapter explores how Christendom's order impacted the lives of women and men through three dynamics: the division between clergy and laity; the relationship of family, church and state; and church regulation of sex and sexuality. To set the scene, we first look at how transformative the Christendom shift was for the church as it moved from the margins to the centre of social and political life and understood itself to be the guardian of truth in an empire where error had no right.

From Margins to Centre

To help understand the background to these instrumental changes that affected the lives of women and men, it is useful to look at the broader picture of the Christendom shift and some other examples of its impact on Christian belief and behaviour.

The realignment of church and empire that occurred with the dawn of what became known as Christendom is vividly illustrated by the changes in the relationship of Christians to the state military. The Christians' widespread refusal to serve in the Roman army was not simply because they would not worship the Roman gods, but because they would not kill.[3] Many early Christians embodied their opposition to bloodshed by not serving in the military. According to Roland Bainton, 'From the end of the New Testament period to the decade of AD 170–180 there is no evidence whatever of Christians being in the Army.'[4] He argues it is probable that abstention from army service was taken for granted in the church and hence there are no church statements during that time prohibiting Christians' military involvement.[5] After this period there is evidence of Christians enrolled in the army, although it is not possible to quantify their involvement. This change in practice is matched by specific instructions from Christian writers against joining the military.

Christian leaders in the third century were quite clear that warfare was incompatible with Christian profession. For Tertullian, writing in 211, on becoming a believer, a man must leave the army, which he stated many had done.[6] The *Traditio Apostolica*, also from the early third century, allowed existing soldiers to begin instruction in Christian faith only if they promised not to kill. If they did take life or if a civilian catechumen or baptized Christian joined the military, they were to be rejected because in doing so they had despised God.[7] Similarly at the beginning of the fourth century, the Christian apologist Lactantius declared Christians should not enter military service, stating it was always wrong to kill.[8] For this stance, some lost their lives. In 295, 21-year-old Maximilian was executed for his refusal to serve in the army. 'I cannot serve as a soldier;' he said, 'I cannot do evil. I am a Christian.'[9] As Arnobius wrote a decade or so later, Christians had learned from the precepts and laws of Christ 'to shed our own blood rather than to stain our hands and conscience with the blood of another'.[10] Even in 336, two decades on from the legalization of Christianity, Martin of Tours, who was baptized while enlisted in the Roman army, left the army when it was due to be engaged in combat.[11]

In the first three centuries, Christians who would not kill were themselves being killed because of their faith. Each century saw particular periods of intense persecution initiated by emperors that took away the Christians' possessions, freedom and often lives. An abrupt change occurred at the beginning of the fourth century when in 312 the emperor Constantine chose not simply to tolerate but to favour Christianity as the religion of the empire and thereby end the persecution of Christians and set a precedent that nearly all subsequent emperors followed. Coming as it did in the context of 'the bloodiest, most destructive persecution Roman officials had ever inflicted on the Christian Church',[12] Constantine's decision came as a great relief to the church.

The seeds of Christendom that were planted with Constantine's legitimization of Christianity, however, changed the church's previous uncompromising stance against taking life. By the second half of the fourth century, stringent proscriptions against involvement in combat situations were absent from the instruction for enquirers and new believers. As early as 314, probably a gesture of reciprocity to Constantine for his decriminalizing of Christianity a year earlier, the Synod of Arles barred soldiers refusing to serve in the army in peace time from receiving the Lord's Supper. In 324 when Constantine went to fight Licinius, his one outstanding imperial rival, bishops, dressed in full regalia, prayed to God on behalf of Constantine's army. For John Chrysostom in Antioch in the 380s, 'Military service presents no hindrance to virtue for the man who is willing to be sober.'[13] Athanasius (also fourth century) believed, 'It is not lawful to kill. But to destroy adversaries in war is legal and worthy of praise.'[14] And in 416, one hundred years on from the turning point of Christians going from being outlawed as part of a minority, illicit, superstitious religion to an accepted and increasingly favoured part of the empire, an imperial edict determined that only Christians could join the army. It was also in the fifth century that Augustine articulated a Christian just war concept that influenced the church throughout the centuries and continues to do so in present post-Christendom times. The swords that at the beginning of the second century had, according to Justin Martyr, been turned into ploughshares, and spears into implements of tillage, three hundred years later were weapons of war once more.

The mainstreaming of Christianity into the empire is further reflected in the imperial pattern of administration that was taken up for church organization. The geographical division into dioceses copied the system established by the emperor Diocletian. The imagery of bishops presiding like imperial magistrates over their domains is reflected in the church's adoption of the Latin terms for chair (*sedes* and *cathedra* giving the English see and cathedral) to refer to a bishop's domain and principal church. And bishops were built grand new churches from state funds from which to preside. These churches, modelled on the audience hall of a secular ruler, evoked the splendour of the court of heaven. 'It was an age when clergy began to dress to reflect their special status as the servants of the King of Heaven. The copes, chasubles, mitres, maniples, fans, bells, censers of solemn ceremony throughout the Church from East to West were all borrowed from the daily observances of imperial and royal households. Anything less would have been a penny-pinching insult to God.'[15]

Clergy took on the elevated status of state officials, and began living in stately villas that reflected their new standing. As pagan priests had before them, Christian bishops and priests received salaries from the state and were no longer supported by voluntary contributions.[16] In addition, the church prospered financially by Constantine making it legal for catholic churches to receive bequests of property, land and other legacies, giving various churches the new experience of longer-term financial security.[17]

Generally, from 312 onwards, the fortunes of Christians improved. Many Christians were allowed to return from exile and had their confiscated property restored, and martyrs' families received financial compensation from the state.[18] Sunday became the universal day of rest across the empire, enabling Christians everywhere to attend worship. Christianity became increasingly respectable, giving those who professed Christian faith religious and social advantages over those who did not.

Christianity and Christians were mainstream. As far as the state was concerned, their faith was no longer an impediment in their social mobility, economic prosperity or overall wellbeing. This new found favour was welcomed by the church, as it brought to an end the terrible persecutions they had been suffering. Constantine's belief that proper reverence to the one God brought the greatest possible benefit to the state was matched by church leaders' convictions that Constantine's actions were authorized by God.

Error Has No Right

Orthodoxy – 'right' thinking and believing – took on particular characteristics within Christendom. Of course, the desire to be faithful to the good news of Jesus was a key concern of the church long before Constantine. In the second century, Christian communities were appearing throughout the Roman world, encompassing at least eighty days of travel.[19] As the gospel message encountered a variety of cultural and religious backgrounds and different personalities, it is not surprising that there was some variance in Christian understanding and practice. In the previous chapter we saw an indication of church leaders' attempts to have conformity on certain matters of belief and practice. One difficulty that disagreements among Christians created for the church in general was the appearance of falsehood that it represented to some of Christianity's critics. Celsus, for example, thought that the only thing the Christians had in common was their name, given the numerous factions they were divided into and the way they detested each other.[20] Accounting for the truth of what they believed and embodying that belief in the way they lived was important for Christians, in part, in order to refute false testimony against them.

At times, the felt need to establish truth from falsehood about the nature of Christian faith was prompted by political events. One example is the impetus by Christian leaders to distinguish themselves from the Jews and hence avoid the imperial retribution following Jewish revolts in the first half of the second century.[21] At the same time, the church was continuing to wrestle with the distortion of Jewish ideas found in Gnosticism.[22] Combating gnostic claims was one reason behind the work of identifying authentic writings about Jesus by those who knew him. These writings could be relied upon as true and genuine and distinct from other works that were not similarly reliable or trustworthy. The prevailing politics meant that negative or erroneous opinion could have serious consequences for Christians. The persecution against Christians in 303 was fuelled, in part, by severe criticism of their religion by the Greek writers, criticism that was addressed at length in the prolific work of the church historian Eusebius.[23]

This drive to clarity and trustworthiness should not be confused with a lack of openness to any discussion or debate. According to David Dungan, the scholar Origen's reply to Celsus' criticism of factions among Christians was to say: 'in so many words, what's so bad about that?'[24] For Origen, writing in the first half of the third century, different schools of thought (*haireseis* from which the term heresy is derived) were inevitable in any matter of import and benefit to human life and 'the wisest Christian was he who had carefully studied the *haireseis* both of Judaism and Christianity'.[25] Even in ascertaining which of the circulating writings were apostolic in authorship, Eusebius (writing in the first quarter of the fourth century) distinguished four kinds of sources: those works that all church leaders acknowledged as genuine; those well-known writings whose origins were disputed by church leaders while accepted by many; other less well-known writings that regardless of orthodox content were considered of spurious authorship; and those writings clearly rejected by all as inauthentic.

Orthodox content, apostolic authorship, and evidence of use by church leaders in apostolic succession for theology and govern-ance in the churches served as the threefold test of authenticity.[26]

As noted in the previous chapter, issues about the authority of apostolic succession created tension and dispute among Chris-tians. Even some who were considered orthodox in their beliefs nevertheless became positioned outside of catholic orthodoxy because of disputes over claims to authority. There was, however, no use of state law or military might to enforce these boundaries of inclusion and exclusion; this was something that would change with the dawn of Christendom.

The unity of the churches was important in Constantine's adop-tion of Christianity for he believed agreement was instrumental to securing the favour of the one God. As emperor, Constantine simply adhered to the traditional Roman imperial pattern of taking responsibility for the religion of the state, which was now in effect Christianity or, more accurately, a catholic Christianity in the sense of mainstream orthodoxy. Constantine's involvement is epitomized in Eusebius' description of him as a 'universal bishop'. Constantine called and directed the business of church councils. Ironically, the first two he initiated, Rome in 313 and Arles in 314, sought to resolve the dispute within the North African church which had arisen, in part, over differences about the fallout for the church of the recent Great Persecution. The issue was whether forgiveness was possible for those who had renounced their faith under persecution, and who was a worthy leader with the authority to offer that forgiveness. A disputed episcopal election in Carthage resulted in two contenders for bishop, with both church councils supporting Caecilian. Other bishops, however, suspected Caecilian of either being ordained by, or being himself, a traditor (someone who handed over copies of Scriptures during perse-cution). They therefore elected an alternative candidate (Major-inus) who was succeeded by Donatus. The Donatists' refusal to accept the two councils' decision about who should be bishop led to Constantine ordering their leaders into exile and confiscating their churches. This had to be enforced militarily, resulting in the death of one Donatist bishop and thus becoming the 'first official persecution of Christians by Christians'.[27]

In the decades that followed, so-called heretical Christian groups had their places of worship and their books confiscated and were banned from public acts of worship. Similarly, pagan rituals were outlawed and their temples stripped of their statues, gold and silver. Pagan worship became what Christian worship had once been – a proscribed *superstitio*, an outlawed religion. The same edict that meant only Christians could join the army (issued in 416) also outlawed pagans from the civil service. Then in 529 the emperor Justinian issued an edict making conversion – including the baptism of all infants – compulsory. The Jews were the one exception to this compulsion, at times being tolerated, at other times persecuted, but always being constructed as other. For everyone else, Christianity became mandatory. As Augus-tine said, 'For long, Christians did not dare answer a pagan; now, thank God, it is a crime to remain a pagan.'[28]

At Constantine's bidding, the collection of authentic, disputed, spurious and rejected Christian texts (as identified by Eusebius) was reduced to a limited number which became solidified into the legal framework of a canon of Scripture, as did the Christian creed, bringing as a consequence 'the enforcement of both with the full power of the Roman government'.[29] Scriptural authenticity became a matter of legality, backed up by the force of the state, and justified by Augustine on the basis that 'error has no right'.

Dissent from orthodoxy, including that which involved prominent women as bearers of authority, was no longer tolerated. Women's equal participation with men of the persecuted church in early Christian martyrdom was not reciprocated in their equal participation in the order of the imperial and persecuting church of Christendom.

Clergy and Laity

The story of clericalism separated from laity is an evolving one through the history of the church. The distinctiveness of church leaders that had been developing throughout the third century took on new meaning in the first centuries of Christendom. In an empire made up almost entirely of Christian subjects, the contrast of a spiritual life with a profane one was no longer between the church and the world but between clerical elites and the laity. This contrast reached definitive expression in the second millennium with ecclesiastical rulers employing exacting means to enforce the idea of an exclusively male and celibate clergy in order to consolidate church influence. For the story of a separated and ultimately exclusively male clerical class is also a story inexorably entangled with attitudes about human sexuality and concerns over wealth and power.

Talk of clericalism is not to be confused or equated simply with debates about ordination, at least not for the first centuries of Christendom. As Gary Macy has shown, the notion and practice of ordination from the twelfth century on was different from that of earlier centuries.[30] Ordination initially referred not to a clerical state but to the process and ceremony by which a person was appointed to any new ministry or *ordo* in the community. Used interchangeably with consecration and benediction, ordination applied not only to bishops, priests and deacons but also to a range of ministries including deaconesses, presbyterae,[31] episcopae,[32] abbesses, canonesses, virgins, widows, nuns, librarians, and even kings, queens, emperors and empresses. This understanding of ordination, which applied to women and men, changed in the twelfth century with a new theology of church orders consisting of a threefold progression of deacon, priest and bishop becoming established, although not without any dispute. The issue pivoted around the presence of deaconesses and abbesses, thought to be the same ministry by different names. While minority scholastic opinion was that these women were ordained, the majority winning position by the thirteenth century was that not only could women not be ordained, but also that they never had been. Further, on account of their female sex, their ordination was impossible. Ordination was no longer practised as recognition of and dedication to a particular ministry by women and men, but as a permanent ordination to a particular status for ministry at the altar, specifically the consecration of bread and wine during the liturgy in order to make the risen Christ present, which was only possible for men. This understanding obfuscates the practice of the church in the first half of the Middle Ages and was accompanied by 'a process of expunging the memory of ordained women from Christianity'.[33]

Common to all women and men ordained to various ministries in the church in the early Middle Ages was the increasing need not only for sexually chaste lives, but also for lives that renounced sexual activity altogether. Advocating celibacy as a human path was not an innovation of the church, nor did it begin for the church only in Christendom. However, the embrace of sexual abstinence by early Christians as an expression of their eschatological hope of a new creation morphed in successive generations into an idea of celibacy associated with cultic purity. The earlier expectation of the imminent return of Jesus which had made social and physical reproduction redundant was revised as the gospel spread, the years went by, and Christian communities and households became established. At first, however, it was the same sexual fidelity, restraint and (post-marital) renunciation expected within all Christian marriages that was required by church leaders, not a forgoing of marriage altogether. But the need for distinctiveness of leaders in contrast to wealthy benefactors of Christian communities, combined with the continuing struggles in understanding human sexual nature, fostered the idea of religiously elite leaders whose calling was incompatible with sexual activity.

The Spanish Synod of Elvira at the beginning of the fourth century ordered bishops, priests, deacons and all clerics attending to the service at the altar to refrain from sexual relations with their wives and to have no more children, failure to do so resulting in expulsion from the priesthood. Subsequent synods gave inconsistent instructions, variously advocating clergy as married, married but sexually continent (which could mean living separately or being chaperoned by fellow clerics), or unmarried. The increasing move by popes to enforce married priests in the Western church to put away their wives clashed with the decision by the Eastern church to allow priests who were married at the time of their ordination to remain with their wives. The decisive Byzantium Trullan Synod in 692 stated that, while those unmarried clerics were to remain so, married deacons and priests who dismissed their wives on the pretext of piety would be excommunicated and, if not amending their behaviour, would be discharged. While bishops' wives were to be cloistered in a distant monastery, a bishop was nevertheless to continue to take care of his wife.[34] This matter of the validity of clerical marriages was a significant point of schism between church traditions in the east and west, before their decisive separation in 1054.

Despite continuing instructions from successive Western popes for a sexually abstemious priesthood separated from women, along with punitive consequences for disobedience, in practice, around the year 1000, 'the majority of clerics seem to have been married'.[35] In the following four centuries, the considerable number of medieval synods speaking out against the marriages of priests indicates how widespread the practice of marriage was among clerics. Unless a priest lived in a monastic community who either shared household work or had servants for the purpose, 'he could scarcely survive without the services of a woman who could cook, clean, spin, weave, make candles, and grow vegetables and herbs. Women provided the domestic economy on which the household depended.'[36]

In the first generations of Christians, it was the existence of sexually abstemious Christian women – older widows of wealth (as distinct from widows in need of church support) – who were patrons of local Christian gatherings that threatened the distinction between leaders and members and hence the inherent matter of influence of church affairs. With Christendom's merging of religious and civic authority, this particular power struggle became a determining factor in shaping clericalism in the new millennium.

The eleventh-century reform movement (of Pope Gregory VII and others) sought to strengthen the position of the church over noble and royal families. By ensuring that appointments to church offices were determined by ecclesiastical regulations and not bestowed by secular elites on family members or allies, the church consolidated control not only of its clergy but also of the associated church land, property and income. The requirement for clerical celibacy further ensured that church wealth would not be diluted through family inheritance. The offspring that priests continued to beget were viewed as illegitimate and, in theory if not always in practice, not entitled to inherit. At the same time, landowners consolidated their own positions, keeping family estates intact, by tightening the system of male primogeniture and patrilineage, which in itself impacted the relationship of women and men with its further disempowering effect on women. 'To put it crudely, the knight and the priest, both in newly-defined roles, conspired to preserve the continuity of aristocratic power through land-holding at the expense of their womenfolk.'[37] It was, of course, the peasantry, both women and men, who continued to bear the brunt of the feudal system.

As with earlier centuries, despite the patriarchal dominance in the church that sought to control and exclude women, this was not the whole story. Women served in local congregations as deacons and deaconesses up until the sixth century after which, in Western churches, women tended to minister more within monastic settings, many of which were privately funded and operated by wealthy families. In Eastern churches deaconesses continued to function within congregations up until the ninth century. In the sixth century, there were 40 deaconesses in the cathedral in Constantinople among its more than 500 officers. In the seventh and eighth centuries abbesses ruled double monasteries consisting of nuns and monks. In the seventh century, Abbess Hilda trained men in the scriptures, including Bosa who became Archbishop of York. Abbesses would hear nun's confessions, preach and distribute communion. As the millennium turned, however, women's ministries became increasingly cloistered and abbesses lost their relative power.[38]

As deaconesses and nuns, women variously cared for the sick and needy, ministered to women helping them at their baptism, assisted with service at the altar and distributed the sacraments. Sanctioned in this by some local clergy, other ecclesiastical offices and synods were vociferous in their opposition, such as: complaints about the 'priestly service' of women;[39] anger about the contempt for divine truths that 'everything that is exclusively entrusted to the service of men has been carried out by the sex that has no right to do it';[40] dismay that divine worship has fallen into 'such disdain that women have presumed to serve at the sacred altars';[41] comment on the shameful presence of women around the altar who 'touch the holy vessels, hand the clerics the priestly vestments, indeed even dispense of the body and blood of the Lord to the people';[42] or disapproval of the 'plague' of nuns touching the holy vessels and sacred linen.[43]

Ecclesiastical authorities issued prohibitions on women's ministry, banning women from the sanctuary, from the baptistery and attending baptisms, and from singing in church. The Synods of Orange in 441, Epaon in 517 and Orléans in 533 all prohibit the ordination of women as deacons and, seven centuries later, Pope Innocent III forbade abbesses to hear confessions, preach, and bless their own nuns.

By the thirteenth century the formal expulsion of women from the lives of male clerics had been achieved. Uta Ranke-Heinemann identifies two significant developments in attempts to enforce a celibate priesthood in the Western church. In 1139 Pope Innocent II declared clerical ordination a diriment impediment to marriage – meaning that the ordained state in itself rendered any marriage null and void. Then in the sixteenth century, mirroring the practice of Martin Luther and other Protestant Reformers, the Counter-Reformation Council of Trent's (1545–63) introduction of a mandatory formal marriage requiring priests and witnesses brought an end to Catholic marriages that could be entered into privately on the basis of the couple's consent and then kept secret. 'Thus after 1139 it was impossible for priests to marry, and after Trent it was impossible for married men to become priests.'[44]

Despite escalating punishment threats of admonishment, salary reduction, loss of parish revenue, complete fiscal confiscation, dismissal, and finally excommunication, the Council of Trent did not succeed in enforcing celibacy any more than previous synodal pronouncements had. However, after Trent many priests continued to live with women as concubines rather than as wives, 'a sad but not infrequently chosen alternative'.[45] Concubines had no rights, and nor, after Pope Innocent II's intervention in the twelfth century, did those women married to priests given that their marriages were considered impossible. These women were designated concubines and whores by Pope Alexander III and adulteresses by Pope Innocent III. Even before this, at a Roman synod in the eleventh century, Pope Leo IX enslaved the wives of priests to the Lateran palace, and a London synod in 1108, also attempting to enforce celibacy, declared priests' wives to be the property of the bishop. Priests' children were viewed as illegitimate. Several church decrees indicated selling priests' children into slavery as a punishment.

The sexual segregation of a male celibate priesthood built on negative views of women. While sex was associated with impurity, 'sexuality and impurity were identified with women'.[46] Women's biology itself was defective, but not only her flesh. Women were considered fickle and flighty and incapable of making sound judgements. Women were thought to lack the intellectual capacities of men and be incapable of engaging in the scholastic enterprises that burgeoned in the late Middle Ages, based in the new universities that replaced monasteries as centres of learning. Hence, women were removed from the sphere of Western Europe's intellectual life. Women were viewed as the polar opposites of men in every respect. 'Women were in effect considered to be monsters. Unnatural in birth, incompetent in mind, and disgusting in their bodily functions, they were clearly inferior to men.'[47]

The distinction between clergy and laity or, more accurately, the spiritual and social hierarchy of clergy and laity, impacted the relationship between women and men in two ways in particular. First, while the need for sexual renunciation was a requirement for both women and men, femaleness, as we shall see further below, bore the heavier burden and guilt for the fact of human sexual nature. While applicable to men as well as women, the paradigm of the sexual body as an inhibitor to spiritual standing and living placed the greater culpability upon women as those who were unclean and hence antithetical to holiness.

Second, the move to an exclusively male priesthood was on the basis that sexual renunciation in itself was not sufficient qualification for women to be included. Rather the fact of female embodiment served as a disqualification from clerical office, an embodiment that was deemed not only dangerously sexually impure, but also morally, intellectually and spiritually inferior to males. This was an assessment that affected not only those women who were denied or might otherwise have been drawn to various forms of ministry that were now reserved exclusively for men. It also impacted on the lives of all women, infiltrating the mindsets and practices of clerical elites who now held the power of salvation.

Family, Church and State

The Catholic Church's renewed insistence on a celibate male priesthood as exemplified by the Council of Trent's stringent measures to discipline non-compliant clergy was, in no small part, a response to the Protestant Reformation's rejection of clerical celibacy in favour of family life.

There had always been families, of course, and marriage was one of the seven sacraments of the Catholic Church. But the prevailing church view at the start of the sixteenth century was that celibacy and virginity were superior to the married state. Sex and sin were inextricably linked and, while not of necessity to be avoided by the laity, the inevitable lust, pollution and disorder of the sex-act was incompatible with the cultic purity required of those who represented Christ.

As part of Martin Luther's intent on unmasking what he saw as the falsehood of the Catholic Church's teaching about salvation, he also argued for – and enacted by getting married – an alternative to priestly celibacy. Marriage was not only a possible option for priests, it was the norm and had been ordained by God as part

of the natural order for the purposes of procreation and companionship. What is more, in a fallen world, it was necessary in order
to contain human sexual lust, which otherwise would lead to sin.

The taking up of marriage by Reformation clergy brought a new
emphasis and attention to the family and in particular the role of
the father as the *paterfamilias* (the male authoritative head) of the
household. For the companionship envisaged would be achieved
by the proper ordering of gender relationships in the household
– with wives being subordinate to their husbands. In Protestant
rhetoric, following the model of the clergy family, it was the father
who was to lead family prayers, replacing the place of the mother
in providing religious instruction to her children. While the Virgin
Mary remained an important figure for mainstream Protestant
Reformers, revered as the mother of Christ albeit stripped of much
of the cultic attachments of pilgrimages and imagery, she was
replaced as a model of Christian faithfulness by Abraham. Many
leading Reformation clergy grew beards as a visual representation
of their biblical patriarchal status and, in so doing, affirming their
male authority in both family and church.

The transition to marriage as not only acceptable but also as
expected was not straightforward for those involved. There were
ambiguities in the new emphasis, particularly for women. On the
one hand, the affirmation of marriage and maternity gave new
positive meaning to women as wives and mothers. Their work
and role was now seen as valid, indeed a vocation recognized
for its own merits. This acknowledgement initially came slowly,
with many of the first wives (often former nuns) of the Reformers
being viewed in popular consciousness as priests' concubines. But
through exhibiting exemplary wifely obedience and charitable
households, they came to represent the ideal commonwealth.

On the other hand, women's horizons shrank to the realm of
the household and they lost the status and relative independence
of alternative community life women had experienced in religious
orders. In convents women had managed property and their own
financial affairs, engaged in learning and spiritual practices for
themselves and others, and provided care and charity for the sick
and poor. In being a tangible display of the Catholic Church's
view of celibacy as a higher vocation than marriage, religious
women defied the Reformation stance of marriage and mother-

hood as women's only legitimate vocation, and their control of their own affairs defied male headship, so much a cornerstone of the Reformers' vision. With the Reformers closing or limiting convents, many nuns had little option but to marry.

The Reformation conviction of the priesthood of all believers may have afforded women and men a similar spiritual standing, but it did not translate to an overturning of patriarchal gender norms. Protestant women who initially engaged in preaching and publishing were met with resistance and were expected to practise their devotion in private, not in public. Many cities stopped women getting together to discuss religion. In England in 1543, an Act of Parliament prohibited women of the nobility and gentry from reading the Bible out loud to others, and all other women from reading it at all.[48] For a patriarchal gender order was part of the means whereby the Reformation gospel would be realized. And this was all to take place with a reconstructed Christendom the Reformers sought to build with the help of secular (that is, not of religious orders) rulers rather than the authorities within the Catholic Church.

The fifteenth and sixteenth centuries were times of change in the economic, cultural and political landscapes of Christendom, which exacerbated social divisions between women and men. The guilds that developed in the growing cities to regulate the skills and production of various crafts increasingly marginalized women, relegating them to low-paid and unpaid work away from skilled production. The renewed use of Roman law, which assumed female inferiority and mental incapacity, negatively impacted women because law-makers selected from provisions that restricted women's rights rather than safeguarded them. The revival of Aristotelian ideas about women's ineligibility for political office or responsibility because they were believed to be irrational creatures excluded women from formal politics. If that were not reason enough, marriage itself was cause to keep women (including widows and unmarried women because they might well marry) from public roles, for their primary duty in obeying their husbands conflicted with independent political action. 'Even to imagine women as political actors, was to reverse the categories of political life, to envisage a world where women ruled men.'[49] Politics was a masculine enterprise with the political citizenry made up of those who, in willingness to defend their cities, annually swore civic oaths of allegiance and bore arms, two things not open to women. Alongside this masculine military image of political inclusion was the notion of fatherhood, both literal and metaphorical.

The renewed family emphasis in rejection of virginity and celibacy made the father-led family the dominant model of social and political organization. For the Reformers, marriage might no longer have been a sacrament, but its importance was in being 'an icon of the social order where the role of the father was a microcosm of the role of a prince as father of his people'.[50] Kings were seen as the husbands and fathers of their people, ruling over them, for the state was like a household, the analogy itself further endowing the authority of male heads of families. Protestant clerical marriages imbued the husband and father role within the family with greater authority because they brought with them the authority of their priestly office. While not discounting the affection that was part of many Reformation marriages, this male authority could be expressed in imprisoning or physically assaulting wives who were considered errant in some way. The idiom 'rule of thumb' originates from the understanding that the diameter of a stick used to beat a wife should not exceed that of a husband's thumb. As Merry Wiesner comments, 'the Protestant elevation of marriage is not the same as, and may in fact directly contradict, an elevation of women *as women*.'[51] Family also became dominant in Protestant church communities; the seating that had been introduced in church buildings (with the Reformation emphasis on listening to the word rather than following a visual drama) becoming occupied according to household.

The hierarchical gender order that underpinned social, political and ecclesial relations meant that, for the most part, for women or men to act outside of their allotted place was viewed as hazardous not only to gender relationships but also to the wellbeing of society as a whole. Such women and men were considered disorderly, meaning they were both outside the social structure and unruly or unreasonable. Women were considered more disorderly than men 'because they were unreasonable, ruled by their physical body rather than their rational capacity, their lower parts rather than upper'.[52] Male rule and female subordination were considered to be the social order given by God and adhering to it was considered necessary for the wellbeing of Christendom.

Sex and Sexuality

Sexual ethics have been a concern of the Christian church from its beginning. The renunciation of sex by many of the first Christians – both outside of and within marriage – was a declaration of their belief that they were living in the last days. Sexual renunciation was a great leveller among people, overturning hierarchies of gender, class and ethnic identity that were bound up in networks of kin-households.

When the new age they anticipated did not come about, successive generations of Christians adapted to their situation through variously adopting, and for some resisting, social patriarchal convention with regard to relationships between women and men in households and communities of believers. Sexual renunciation continued to be an option and found its place among ascetic and prophetic groups and increasingly in the ranks of male clergy who, as expressed by Eusebius, demonstrated 'the perfect form of the Christian life', with a 'secondary piety' being his assessment of those who married and raised children.

As we have seen in this chapter, ensuring the celibacy of its priests was an ongoing struggle for church authorities and part of the contested ground on which the Reformation – and then Counter-Reformation – played out. The Reformation emphasis on family life defined female and male sexuality according to a gender hierarchy that mirrored the proper order of church and state, with family, ecclesial and political male leadership viewed as ordained by God.

Enmeshed in the story of Christian sexual ethics has been a sexual double standard whereby women are viewed as more culpable than men for humanity's sexual failings. In a dualistic mindset that understands the world to consist of pairs of opposites such as active and passive, strong and weak, reason and emotion, dominant and subordinate, spiritual and physical, men have been associated with the former and women the latter, with greater value and esteem given to men and associated male attributes.

Women's presumed passive, weak and material nature was reflected in early physiological understanding that thought the female contributed nothing but a host body to reproduction. The Aristotelian belief that male semen contained the entire human embryo from which new life came influenced a number of church regulations about sex; 'anything which stopped male seed doing its job was an act of murder – from masturbation to contraception to same-sex relations.'[53] It also relegated women in the human story, for maleness was viewed as perfect humanity from which femaleness diverged (see Chapter 4).

Female weakness was also part of the notion of original sin – the inherent disorder of fallen humanity – that was developed by Augustine at the end of the fourth century. For Augustine, the disobedience of human will involved in original sin focused on the inevitability of lust in sexual intercourse, which linked sex to sin. The sex-act itself he viewed for himself and all males to be disorderly, given the lack of control and bodily pleasure it involves which he thought inconsistent with a will seeking after God. While permissible within marriage for reproduction and to prevent fornication, Augustine believed the sex-act is never without lust and hence sin. And the blame for this state of affairs was down to a woman – Eve who first disobeyed God and got Adam to do the same, following which creation fell from its state of perfection. Thus Eve, on behalf of all women since, could be depicted as both morally weak and sexually impure; 'women, sex and sin' being the 'emotional trinity' at the heart of the idea of original sin.[54]

Sexual desire was viewed as a problem for men too, but often seen as an inevitability given the strength of sexual desire. Women bore the responsibility for male sexuality either by providing sexual services through marriage or perhaps prostitution, or by behaving in ways, sometimes by seclusion or covering, so as not to be a temptation to men.

Perceptions concerning women's materiality and moral weakness required their separation not just from men, but also from the holy. The story of the black marble in Durham Cathedral with which this chapter began was replicated in churches throughout the Middle Ages and was rooted in ritual laws of pollution: 'The ranking of a congregation from east to west, placing women farthest from the altar, chancel, and holiest part of the building, rested on deep-seated fears of their impurity . . . the sense of need to protect sacred ground and holy rites went on making fences against the female sex.'[55]

The sexualization of women was an integral part of the witch hunts of the fifteenth and sixteenth centuries that sought to root out, torture and execute women considered to be the devil's hand-maids. Accusations against women who were called bawds and hot whores, and were thought to copulate with the devil, included that they could remove and restore or bewitch a man's genitals, stop male generative power to prevent conception and cause impotence, or seduce virgin women. The *Malleus Maleficarum* stated that all witchcraft came from carnal lust, which it said was insatiable in women. As those naturally more impressionable, women were more prone to the influence of disembodied spirits, which as witches they used for ill and hence were evil.

However, in more recent times, this fragility has been a reason for women needing to be kept in the confines of domesticity, protected from the wider, more aggressive, public world. Women have thus been viewed variously as sexual temptresses, and also as vulnerable, weak and in need of protection – one view ascribing an evil power to women, the other negating their own agency, and both denying women the opportunity for positive self-actual-ization. Instead, these definitions have contributed to the mainte-nance of a patriarchal gender order.

Within Christendom, an ordered sexuality was part of the proper order of all things. But it became a contest about church authority in regard to the clergy, those in religious life, and the lives of the faithful as church leaders struggled to have clergy and laity conform to ecclesial law and regulations.

The contemporary churches' concern with sexual ethics is clearly not a new phenomenon. Yet arguably, in these post-Chris-tendom times of transition, as ecclesiastical institutions are renegotiating their relationship to a diverse, multi-faith and multi-cultural society, it is in the area of sexual identity and behaviour that churches have focused as marks of their own identity. In other words, against a general background of loss of public influence,

the specificity of sexuality has been a defining area of resistance
for the churches against their diminishing role.

Linda Woodhead considers that 'the contemporary churches'
anxiety over the control of sexuality in the modern world has a
great deal to do with their struggle to retain social power in a situation where such power is under increasing threat'.[56] Churches
have concerned themselves with the whole structuring of relations
between the sexes, including the changing roles and expectations
of women and subsequent impact on families, divorce, contraception, abortion, reproductive technologies – heterosexual married
families being seen as the place of reproduction of the faith as
well as of stable society. To a large extent, defending this family
pattern has meant the regulation of women's lives, but it is the
subject of homosexuality and many churches' opposition to it that
has proved the focal point of attention in more recent years. Put
simply, Linda Woodhead argues that a loss of control of public life
led to an intensification of attempts to control domestic life along
with a reaction against modern ' "permissiveness" in the quest for
a distinctive Christian identity in a time of rapid change'.[57]

The impact of a Christendom mindset is still being felt in the
area of gender relations, even as churches contend with losing
their influence in the world. The time of the relationship between
women and men being caught up in struggles over church power
and authority is not yet over.

4.

Equality: A More Just Hermeneutics

The notion of equality profoundly challenges the hermeneutics of order that places people in gender hierarchies. Which is why, of course, equality is embraced by some and regarded with suspicion by others. Rooted in the modern period in the revolutionary and democratic struggles dating from the eighteenth century, the past one hundred years have seen a gradual realignment towards gender equality in attitudes, actions and legislation. The general acceptance of the public rhetoric of equality, however, masks the persistence of continuing gender inequality and also has produced strong reactions in objection that continue to undermine achieving equality more fully. This chapter explores these dynamics, with particular attention to the women's movement(s) and Christian concerns with what has been called the feminization of the church. It also examines men's movements that have arisen in response and asks if these represent innovative ways of relating or a regrouping of the old patriarchal order between women and men that was embedded in Christendom.

Women's Movements

The twentieth-century women's movements for rights and equality have their roots in the political discourse that emerged against the backdrop of Enlightenment philosophy and the French and American Revolutions. In England, the social and political upheaval of the latter part of the eighteenth century sought to reform the assumed power and privilege of aristocratic leadership. It was argued that people had a right to consent to their governing authorities and also to withdraw that consent should that authority be abused. Further, based on the Enlightenment affirmation of human capacity for rationality and the importance of education, the people were equipped to exercise their rights.

By 'people', of course, was meant 'men'. While Thomas Paine's *The Rights of Man* appeared in print in 1791,[1] it was Mary Wollstonecraft who in 1792 published *Vindication of the Rights of Woman* in which she took up the egalitarian principles of the time and applied them to women. Women, she said, shared the capacity of men for rational thought and learning, forming judgements, and living moral lives. She argued for women's emancipation and gave a powerful critique of social and economic systems that kept women ignorant and subordinated to men. It would be seventy-five years, however, until the first parliamentary debate on women's suffrage was held in 1867 when John Stuart Mill, MP, proposed, unsuccessfully, an amendment to the Reform Bill, changing the word 'man' to 'person'. There followed twenty-eight parliamentary bills introducing women's suffrage, all of which failed, before the first women got parliamentary votes in 1918.[2]

The developing discourse on equality and rights that emerged in the midst of revolution and change at the end of the eighteenth century did not include women. Since then women, and on occasions men, have worked to bring about better treatment for women. Successful advancements for women in the nineteenth century included: the setting up of girls' schools; the first women undergraduates being accepted at universities; married women keeping their inheritance; a few women crossing professional barriers to become, for example, doctors and accountants; women householders and hence rate-payers voting in local elections; and women being able to vote and to stand for election for the new school boards established in the 1870 Education Act.[3]

The last one hundred years have seen increasing civil and political equality for women with men in terms of public representation, democratic voice, access to employment, employment terms and conditions, and rights over their own bodies. In 1918, the Parliament (Qualification of Women) Act enabled women aged twenty-one and over to stand for Parliament.[4] Ten years later, in 1928, the Equal Franchise Act gave all women over twenty-one the vote (all men over twenty-one had been enfranchised in 1918 along with women over thirty who were either a householder, the wife of a householder, or had been to university). In 1942, the Trade Union Congress (TUC) pledged itself to the principle of equal pay (which they had first debated in 1888). In 1955 equal pay was agreed for teachers, civil servants and local government officers. Twenty years later, in 1975, the 1970 Equal Pay Act stipulating equal pay for women and men doing the same job came into force. This was supplemented in 1984 with the Equal Value Amendment that allowed women to claim equal pay to men doing similar but different jobs if they were considered to be of equal value. In 1975, the same year that Margaret Thatcher became the first woman leader of a political party in Britain, legislation banned sex discrimination in employment, education and advertising, and made it unlawful to dismiss a woman because she was pregnant. The marriage bar, wherein women were forced to leave their jobs on getting married, was common practice up to the 1960s and it was used in the Foreign Office until 1972, although it had been lifted in the civil service in 1946. In 1991, after more than one hundred years of feminist campaigning and overturning a legal judgement dating back to 1736 that denied the necessity of married women's consent to sex with their husbands, rape within marriage became a criminal offence. All these reforms involved provisions within state, legal and/or social institutions designed to bring about greater equality for women with men.

By the 1960s, however, the language of feminist activism changed from equality and rights to liberation and oppression. These terms reflected the context of political liberation movements of the time and they spoke of the underlying causes of women's inequality and lack of rights; namely, the pervasive social relations of a sex/gender system that operated not only in institutions but also culturally throughout society. This system impacted on the structures and on the mindsets of both women and men. Women were oppressed in a male-defined sex-roles system in which their sense of themselves and social norms about what they could do were shaped by a deterministic view of biological sex. This was a patriarchal system in that it served the needs and desires of men, allocating women a subordinate and dependent role in a sexual division of labour (of reproduction and production) that operated in both private and public domains. What is more, the nature of domestic relations in the private sphere of the family was connected to women's empowerment in the public sphere. Matters of childcare, birth control, economic independence, along with equality in employment and an end to violence against women, were core concerns. Achieving equality involved more than a levelling process between women and men; this was insufficient for the nature of what was wrong. Rather, it required a thoroughgoing reappraisal of the power relations between women and men involving changes in attitudes and actions in all areas of life. The phrase 'the personal is political' arose in this period, known as second-wave feminism, in direct challenge to the public/private dichotomy which operates on the assumption that matters pertaining to the private world are not influenced by, or supportive of, wider social agendas.

While the refusal to give up privilege and power remains a key element in unequal gender relations, the failure to examine how gender operates in society also accounts for the continued inequality that exists between women and men in the twenty-first century.

Rhetoric and Reality

The past one hundred years have seen enormous changes in the lives of women. However, the public rhetoric of equality that we now have and which is reflected in law and policy is far from realized. When women first received parliamentary votes in 1918 there were fears that it would lead to a 'petticoat government'. Yet in 1992, after more than seventy years of women being able to stand for Parliament, only 9 per cent of MPs were women. The difficulty is not with people voting for women, but with women being successful at their party-candidate selection stage. For women's success at this stage, 'the single most influential factor, more than social and cultural issues such as women's professional standing, is the use of measures such as twinning,[5] zipping[6] and quotas'.[7]

In the 1999 elections for the Scottish Parliament and Welsh Assembly the Labour Party adopted twinning of candidates. This resulted in equal numbers of their female and male candidates elected in Scotland and two more Labour women than men being elected in Wales. While in the 2010 general election the Labour Party lost 97 seats, its use of all-women shortlists meant it increased its number of female MPs from 28 to 31 per cent.[8] In total, the 2010 general election saw 22 per cent of women, the largest percentage ever, elected to Westminster. Female government ministers, however, remain a minority. The first government formed by the Liberal Democrat/Conservative coalition had only four women out of twenty-three cabinet ministers making up just 17 per cent. The male dominance of the core executive of British politics (the organization and procedures of cabinet ministers, senior civil servants and senior policy advisors who hold the power of decision-making) means that women are disadvantaged in gaining access to positions of authority and in carrying out their responsibilities.

> [T]he UK core executive has a gendered disposition in relation to its recruitment, roles, access to resources, membership of networks and tactics used by core executive actors. This is the consequence of the traditional exclusion of women and the way the institution interconnects with other institutions such as the family. It may prove harder for politicians and bureaucrats with caring responsibilities, many of whom are women, to access and operate effectively in the male domain that is the core executive.[9]

In 2013, more than four decades after the introduction of equal pay legislation, women in the UK, working full-time, earned on average 15 per cent less per hour than men working full-time. This means that women effectively receive their last pay cheque around the beginning of November and work the majority of the last two months of the year for free.[10] The Fawcett Society identifies three factors that produce this pay gap. First, some employers simply continue to pay women less for doing the same job as men – this discrimination may account for up to 40 per cent of the pay gap. Second, work traditionally done by women (such as cleaning, catering and caring) is still paid less than that done by men (such as construction, transportation and skilled trades); a nurse is paid less than a police officer. This gendered labour segregation and accompanying financial difference reflects the lesser value (both socially and economically) ascribed to women's contributions and those things with which women are associated. Third, the UK has one of the longest working hours' cultures in the EU, so as long as women shoulder the majority of parenting and caring responsibilities, women are unable to compete in the UK workplace. 'Combine this male breadwinner/female carer divide with the resurgence in objectification and sexualization of women and judgement of value on the basis of appearance and you have a potent set of stereotypes that influence the entirety of women's experience in the workplace.'[11]

Having children is a major factor in the gender pay gap with many mothers moving to work part-time, which often means posts at lower grades, with less security and prospects, or in a sector with low pay. 'A cycle exists where mothers' traditional caring roles lead them to leave paid work or to work part-time, which leads to lower remunerations, which reinforces domestic gender roles so that it makes financial sense for fathers rather than mothers to work full-time. This cycle is not inevitable; mothers in countries where labour markets are organized differently face a lower pay penalty.'[12]

In a Jacky Fleming cartoon, a man in a suit and tie sits behind a desk, leaning forward slightly to address the viewer as if they were on the other side of the desk, pen in his hand, with a whimsical look, or perhaps a smirk, on his face. 'Which is it you want', reads the caption, 'equality or maternity leave?'[13] In 2005, the Equal Opportunities Commission estimated that around thirty thousand women lost their jobs each year as a result of becoming pregnant despite the fact that such discrimination became illegal in 1975.[14] The idea that equality in the workplace means that women's physical and social embodiment in the generation of children is a hindrance rests on the patriarchal notion that the normal human body is a male one. Hence, anything that differs from that is an aberration in the workplace, which is designed around a male physical blueprint. This is starkly evident in the uniforms that have been provided for women police officers, which until recently have not been designed around female body shape. Only in the past decade has the practice of making slight amendments to garments designed around male body shape for use by women officers been questioned, including, for example, the practice of women ordering their shirts by collar size.[15]

At the same time as women's physicality is being seen as a hindrance or ignored, their relative status remains ingrained in social perceptions. Women are still referred to by their marital status in terms of formal address. When women are asked their names, it will be followed by the question, 'Is that Miss or Mrs?' In other words, they are being asked, are you single, in all likelihood never married, or are you married, or at least at one time have been even if you are now widowed, separated or divorced? In this question women are being perceived first and foremost as relative beings – relative *to men*. It detracts from women's autonomy as adults, socially locating them primarily not in relationship but in relationship to men in a way that is not involved in reverse in formal address of men. Imagine asking men whether they were married or not, every time they gave their names, and you would have some idea of the interaction that is taking place every time a woman is asked, 'Is that Miss or Mrs?' An alternative would be to use 'Mrs' for all women when they reach eighteen years of age (the age at which people may vote, can purchase alcohol and get married without parental consent).

Many women, of course, enjoy the title 'Mrs', in celebration of being married. 'Mrs' can convey respectability, being a female grown-up, protected, all of which can be positive attributes. It is the wider context of women being treated relative to men and not also men relative to women that gives this social convention its potency in perpetuating maleness as normative humanity. The way society is comfortable with identifying women primarily by their marital status is seen in attitudes towards the title 'Ms' as an alternative to 'Miss' or 'Mrs'. Unsuccessful as a single replacement for the two latter terms, 'Ms' has become associated with women whose marital status is not known, or those who do not fit neatly into single or married categories (those who are separated, divorced or cohabiting). It frequently carries negative associations. It is disliked by many because it is associated with feminism, from which both women and men distance themselves.

However, for other women, 'Ms' is a title that 'gives them the privacy men take for granted'.[16] It is not that women who choose 'Ms' necessarily wish to hide their marital status, although some may. But it is an objection to the inability of society to relate to them without their status being known. As Margaret Gibbon argues,

'The desire to mark women's status relative to men (as unmarried, married, divorced) only makes sense in a patriarchal society where women are not accorded independent status on a par with men and need to have their sexual un/availability signalled.'[17]

The above illustrations give a curious mix of denying women's physicality as female persons and as child-bearers while at the same time perceiving them primarily as females relative to men and children. Yet neither approach scrutinizes the state of gender relations and social structures in private and public life in order to foster the flourishing of 'adequate models of loving and working'[18] which would benefit both women and men, all parents and children.

Men in the Mirror

One response to the women's movements of second-wave feminism was the development of identifiable men's movements that came to prominence in the early 1990s. The critique of patriarchy – a system of constructed male dominance that disadvantaged, indeed oppressed, women – put men's behaviour and male privilege under a spotlight. The male dominance and masculine bias in so many areas of life, which despite being pervasive had largely been obscured from attention, was now being questioned and men found themselves in the unusual position of being subjects of critical inquiry. This critique and attention provoked responses. 'Faced with the daily realities of sharing power with women at home, at work, and in the community, many men have found in the men's movement a place to explore and express dissatisfaction with their changing social position, and confusion about their identities as men.'[19]

One of the best-known responses was the mythopoetic movement that used myth and poetry as tools for male self-discovery and personal development. Against the criticism of hegemonic masculinity (that is, male dominance institutionalized in culture and social practice) and anxieties over the loss of male power, mythopoeticism sought to affirm and rebuild wounded masculinity in the context of the perceived feminization of society. It did so through exploring fatherlessness, male bonding, initiation rites, wildness, and Jungian masculine archetypes (king, warrior, magician and wild man), themes that also feature in some Christian men's ministries.

Mythopoeticism was popularized through Robert Bly's book, *Iron John*,[20] which used the Grimm brothers' fairy tale of Iron John – a wild man who breaks out of an enchanted state by helping the prince in the story through an initiation into manhood – as a parable for modern men. Men were becoming effeminate, 'soft', due to overbearing mothers and female partners, and an absence of male mentoring, particularly fathers. The development of their 'feminine side', a receptivity in which they became more thoughtful and gentle, while valuable in itself, did not make them happy or free. For this they needed to recover the wild man that lies deep within the male psyche.

While aspects of mythopoeticism were welcomed by some women for its therapeutic value of engaging men with their own feelings and encouraging greater emotional self-expression, there was also criticism of the movement (by women and men) as a reclothing of patriarchy that continued to blame women and defend its own privilege. The new masculinity it fostered was founded on separation from women – as both distinct from, and opposite to, women – and it failed to situate male development in families in the wider social context of male public power. It was an inherently personal – not social or political – movement and ignored wider gender power relations. Characteristic of its leaders was 'their emphasis on (white) male intrapsychic self-affirmation in a way that avoids entirely any social awareness of sexism, heterosexism, racism, and class as social injustice'.[21] In particular, it failed to deal with male violence against women. Margaret Randall observed, 'we live in a society where *Women Who Love Too Much* is an instant best seller, while *Men Who Hit Too Much* has yet to be written'.[22]

In contrast, there were some men's initiatives that directly addressed male violence. In 1991, the year throughout which *Iron John* appeared on the *New York Times* bestseller list, men in Canada launched the White Ribbon campaign in response to the mass shooting of fourteen female students in Montreal two years earlier.[23] One hundred thousand men across Canada wore a white ribbon as a symbol of men's opposition to male violence against women. Wearing a white ribbon is a 'personal pledge to never commit, condone or remain silent about violence against women and girls'. [24] It is 'the world's largest male-led movement working to end violence against women and girls, promote gender equity, healthy relationships and a new vision of masculinity',[25] and there are now White Ribbon campaigns in over sixty countries, including the UK.[26]

As well as mythopoetic and pro-feminist men's movements among the responses to second-wave feminism, there were also groups focusing on men's rights and particularly fathers' rights, especially for separated fathers whose children do not live with them. The discourse of fathers' rights groups often presents men as victims of systems that are biased towards women as mothers and against them as fathers. More generally, men's rights groups are focused on the harmful effects of hegemonic masculinity on men rather than on its impact on women and children. Hence, some note, 'Although at its extreme edge the men's rights perspective is sometimes antifeminist and even misogynistic, it is possible, at least in principle, to support both men's rights and a liberal feminist agenda.'[27]

The responses to the women's movement have been wide-ranging. It is only a few who suggest that women have never been discriminated against but rather it is men who are oppressed. There are many who believe that the traditional gender roles of men as providers and protectors and women as carers and nurturers are the natural order that should be supported. Many others agree in principle and practice with gender equality but consider either that equality largely has been achieved and there is no more work to be done or that things have gone too far and unnecessarily so. And there are yet others who continue to see the need for much greater examination and change in social relations between women and men in all areas of life.

A similar spectrum exists among Christians in their reactions to the social changes in the lives of women and men, changes which also impact church life. As many expressions of church within Christendom are far removed from the non-hierarchical gender relations imagined and practised in the earliest churches, many Christians were unprepared for the challenges brought by second-wave feminism. Several decades on, the dominant discourse among Christians in Britain about the changes in social relations between women and men is that of the feminization of the church.

The Feminization of the Church and the Crisis in Masculinity

When people talk of the feminization of the church, they usually mean one of two things. The first is simply that more women go to church than men. This is observable in many if not most congregations although the majority of church leaders continue to be male. However, in the Church of England, who first ordained women to the priesthood in 1994, the number of women clergy continues to rise while the number of male clergy is decreasing (41 and 24 per cent respectively for full-time stipendiary clergy – those financially supported by the church – in the ten years since 2002). In 2012, women made up nearly one third (32 per cent) of all diocesan clergy,[28] although less than a quarter (23 per cent) of full-time stipendiary ministers.[29] A greater number of women are also involved in lay or non-ministerial leadership positions across church denominations than in previous generations. This increasing presence and visibility of women is one meaning of the feminization of the church.

The second meaning is that church has become feminine in its thinking and practice. This is seen in several ways: the emphasis on emotion and feeling in hymns, prayers and worship; the focus on Christian identity as personal relationship with Jesus (rather than adherence to doctrinal beliefs and religious authorities); and the increased attention to caring for church members (by God, church leaders and each other).

Even church buildings are said to have become feminized with children's pictures, flowers and banners. Put another way, those things that are associated with femininity – love, emotional expressivity, nurture, gentleness, focus on and concern for children and family – have become the hallmark values of church, faith and believers. Most importantly for the understanding of feminization, it is not that these aspects are now present having been absent before, but they have replaced the values and characteristics associated with masculinity that have previously defined church and faith. Hence Carl Beech, the general director of the UK men's ministry, Christian Vision for Men, comments, 'Men seek adventure and challenge and whilst love and compassion are important traits for men, the wild and adventurous aspects of their personalities can be completely starved in church.'[30]

Often these two meanings of feminization are said to be related. After all, if more women than men are involved in church, perhaps it is inevitable that increasingly church would reflect the characteristics of its female members. In the light of this feminization, which is viewed as hindering men's participation, a lot of attention and energy is being given to how men might be attracted to and be comfortable within church. The past forty years or so have seen the development of an identifiable, if diverse, men's movement or ministry to men among Christians, in some ways paralleling developments in the wider men's movement.

Probably the best-known Christian men's movement is Promise Keepers in the USA founded in 1990 by Bill McCartney, a football coach at Colorado University. In 1991 their first rally was held, attended by 4,200 men. Over the next twenty years Promise Keepers involved over five and a half million men[31] through its large rallies (well over one million men attended rallies across 22 venues in 1996), smaller localized support groups, and numerous multimedia resources. As dominant in public consciousness as Promise Keepers has been, ten years after its formation one estimate was that there were over 34,000 men's ministries of an evangelical orientation in America,[32] from small independent groups to larger or national organizations. Promise Keepers itself is an evangelical-oriented organization, although ecumenical in its outreach, welcoming Catholic men to its events. Bill McCartney was raised and continued to identify himself as Catholic until he had a conversion experience when he was thirty-three years old, and the organization has encouraged Catholic participation. The United States Conference of Catholic Bishops (USCCB) followed the progress of Promise Keepers with interest and, recognizing its impact, they responded positively and proactively to it by establishing what became known as the National Fellowship of Catholic Men (NFCM) to provide a distinctively Catholic ministry to men, which included sacramental celebration and devotion to the saints.[33]

Many Christian men's movements focus on reaching out to men for the dual purposes of evangelism and discipleship. Sometimes these ministries feature paths to personal growth and development that are Christian parallels to the mythopoetic men's movement. They follow a therapeutic approach, encouraging greater emotional expressivity by and among men that is then taken into family relationships – towards wives and children. Often in men's ministries there is a focus on personal transformation as the means to transform society. There is much emphasis on personal responsibility as leaders in churches and families, being good husbands and fathers, and the importance of men fulfilling their responsibilities for the betterment of society. One Promise Keepers author attributed America's social problems to the feminization of the American male, which he described as 'a misunderstanding of manhood that has produced a nation of sissified men who abdicate their role as spiritually pure leaders, thus forcing women to fill the vacuum'.[34] Christian Men's Network, based in America where it was founded in 1977 by Edwin Louis Cole and which has a small presence in the UK, connects faithful Christian men to strong families, communities and nations: 'When men accept their responsibility to guide, guard, and govern in righteousness both at home and work, stability and strength are provided, vision is maintained and Peace reigns.'[35]

These men's movements and ministries (including a growing body of multimedia resources) are about the intersection of masculinity with a Christian faith which is perceived as feminine. Another way to speak of feminization is to talk in terms of a crisis in masculinity that this feminization has brought about. Men are said to be unsure of who they are either because women have taken away their role and place in society or because men have abdicated this through their own irresponsibility and lost their way. The association of Christian faith with femininity becomes a barrier to men responding to the gospel or inhabiting a faith identity. It is this association that men's movements seek to counter (and arguably in some cases to break altogether) by realigning masculinity and Christianity and making faith a compatible masculine enterprise. No doubt not all men involved in men-only groups would recognize that description, even if it is espoused by the founders and leaders of their organizations. It is, however, this wider context of perceived feminization and questions about male place and identity that has produced the current interest and availability of male-only environments for men to develop in Christian faith.

The popularity and growth of men's ministries indicates that they are meeting perceived need among many men. Many women also welcome such groups for the positive impact they have on the men in their lives. However, rather than accepting without question this particular narrative account of feminization and its consequences, further consideration of the phenomenon shows we need different ways to think about being women and men together in churches after Christendom.

Feminization Re-Examined

Talk of the feminization of the church is not new. Discussions about how many women were attracted to Christianity and the accompanying implications for masculinity arose in the eighteenth century. Industrialization had led to the division between the public world of industry, politics and business as a male domain, and the private world of domesticity, gentility and children, populated by women. The public world was one of male power, a power that was increasingly shared by men in the rising middle class who sought definition and significance in enterprises in the public world that took them outside of their homes both phys-ically and emotionally. At the same time, the church, no longer having a monopoly on public life, slowly began to lose its influ-ence and became relocated into the private sphere. Increasingly (particularly middle-class) women became moral guardians of the household providing a private haven for their men from the more brutal public world of business, a role endorsed in the nineteenth century by churches advocating a particular gendered Christian piety for women. This ascribed role of woman as the 'angel in the house' extended beyond home life to churches, charitable enter-prises and social organizations, giving many middle-class women outlets for some of their skills and abilities beyond the confines of their homes. Concerns that men would be alienated further from churches which were increasingly female-populated and which had much of their activity – both social and missionary – sustained by women went alongside a diminishing status of both churches and clergymen, and were mutually exacerbating factors.

Fears that churchgoing and religious faithfulness were considered unmanly led to a focus on strong, vigorous, masculine accounts of Christianity from the second half of the nineteenth century – called variously 'muscular Christianity' or an emphasis on the physical and moral virtues of 'manliness'. Connected to anxieties that physically weakened and effeminate men would be unfit to fight for the British Empire, manhood was redefined by melding male physicality to spirituality and emphasizing militaristic and sporting activities. Boys' organizations such as Boy Scouts and Boys' Brigade are an early twentieth-century expression of muscular Christianity. More recent publications, such as Edwin Louis Cole's 1982 *Maximized Manhood*, Patrick Arnold's 1991 *Wildmen, Warriors and Kings*, and John Eldredge's 2001 *Wild at Heart: Discovering the Secret of a Man's Soul*, that have been written about contemporary Christian masculinity have forebears in Thomas Hughes' 1879 publication *The Manliness of Christ*, and S.S. Pugh's 1867 *Christian Manliness: A Book of Examples and Principles for Young Men*.[36] Fears about feminization are not new.

It is also true that any discussion of feminization is possible only because of the acceptance that humanity consists of two sexes. As obvious as that may seem, throughout the church's history before the Enlightenment, the prevailing understanding was that perfect humanity was male, and women were underdeveloped men. It is this thought that underpins earlier ideas about women attaining higher spiritual standing by losing their femaleness in order to become like men. This one-sex model of humanity was replaced by a two-sex model, which viewed women and men as two distinct sexes each with their own virtues and values. Crucially, male and female were set in opposition to one another in this understanding and, while their values could complement each other, this was still a patriarchal concept, for power and authority were considered male attributes.[37] This emphasis on sexual difference was not incidental to eighteenth-century equality and rights discourse, but a means to continue women's inequality on the basis of a fundamental difference between the sexes. Women's physical and intellectual character was said to determine their unsuitability for the democratic rights being given to men.[38]

This move from the one-sex to the two-sex model of humanity shows that any feminization of (in this case) the church is not a move from some gender-neutral (assuming that were possible) or gender-inclusive understanding of normative humanity, but from a masculine one. So the narrative of feminization is also the narrative of changing masculinity. So-called feminization occurs when women enter what has been masculine space (physical or cultural); the subsequent so-called crisis in masculinity results as men are forced to adjust to the changing position of women in church, home and society. Of interest here is the extent to which attempts addressing this feminization that focus on re-masculin-izing the church, Christian thinking and behaviour (variously through Christian men's movements and literature) are not moving beyond Christendom's order but finding new ways to maintain it.

Changing language is one indicator of an adapting Chris-tendom order. As a focus on women's social equality became increasingly visible, this directly challenged a patriarchal gender hierarchy. As a result, the language of male dominance and female subordination became increasingly unacceptable, being replaced by terms such as (servant) leadership and submis-sion respectively to describe what were said to be natural and God-given gender norms. Similarly, in the 1970s and 1980s, the terms hierarchical and liberation were applied to the views of male authority over women and the counteraction of that idea,[39] but subsequently the terms used are more likely to be comple-mentarian and egalitarian respectively.[40] For both viewpoints, this reflects a change in language that is more in keeping with social sensibilities in an age that adopts the public rhetoric of female equality. The proponents of male authority now stress male responsibility rather than male rule, and complementarity evokes a sense of partnership and working with the strengths of each for the best of everyone rather than any notion of men 'lording' it over women. Nonetheless, a divinely ordained male authority over women remains the distinguishing feature of this view. Various commentators have described this re-invention of the old idea of gender hierarchy in terms of 'soft patriarchy',[41]

'soft-boiled masculinity',[42] 'neopatriarchy',[43] 'last gasp patriarchy',[44] and 'patriarchy in the last instance'.[45]

A religious discourse of gender hierarchy is incompatible with
the current public discourse of gender equality. The main focus
for the former therefore is church and family life. The idea that
this reduces its sphere of influence, while accurate, is misleading.
As Linda Woodhead points out, private domestic space – where
women and men invest the greater part of their hopes, fears and
indeed money – is the sphere 'most important in the construction of men's and (particularly) women's identity', and the place
in which the next generation is formed and nurtured.[46] In addition, given the place of the family as the foundation of society or
bedrock of nations, especially within conservative formulations,
both religious and secular, the perpetuation of patriarchal gender
relationships in private and family life has wider social and political impact. On a practical level, parenting, other care-giving
and housework arrangements in the home are influential in how
family members participate outside the home. Gender-defined
roles and expectations also shape personal development, expectations and the creation of opportunities.

The renewed emphasis on a masculine role within families and
households may also be a response to men losing economic power
and employment status because of the changes and challenges to
employment and income in a global economy that has also been
experiencing recession. Alongside the public rhetoric of gender
equality, decreasing socio-economic power means that the family
is replacing work as the focus for male identity and purpose. The
increased involvement of men in the domestic sphere and the call
for a greater work–life balance may well be connected to this relo-
cating of male identity to home and family. If increasingly home
is the place where men find affirmation for male identity that they
are losing through employment, they will want to adjust the allocation of their time and energy between work and home to invest
more where they find significance. The idea that male-led households are the means to ensure social stability and wellbeing also
imbues men with a sense of wider social influence.

Integral to much of the new masculinity discourse is the place
and role of men as fathers. The emphasis on more engaged
fathers has been welcomed by many who overlook any (implicit

or explicit) patriarchal control in view of the benefits of having men's greater participation in family life. However, discussing two men's ministries specifically for fathers, one Catholic and one evangelical, Joseph Gelfer points out that their fundamental theme is not necessarily Christian *fatherhood* but Christian *men*. He argues that men are the focus of these organizations into which fatherhood has been co-opted.[47]

The place of children, who are so heavily identified as being part of women's sphere and work, is one indication of the extent to which the construction of this new masculinity is breaking away from previous oppositional gender norms. If involved 'hands-on' parenting is part of male Christian responsibility and indeed pleasure there should be no reason to see children's pictures and play areas in church settings, for example, as creating a feminine environment. Or is masculinity still being constructed or understood in a way that requires separation from the material world of children?

Crucial in the construction of this new masculinity is a tendency to conflate manliness with godliness or Christlikeness. 'Manhood and Christlikeness are synonymous' is core to the message of the Christian Men's Network.[48] In contrast to the 'traditional approach', which 'has been to seek to emasculate Jesus in an attempt to find a divinely androgynous ideal', some argue for Jesus to serve as 'the ultimate archetype for men as men'.[49] While this archetype understands Jesus to give up male power through his death thereby setting men free from conventional masculinity, it also, whether consciously or not, makes the fact that Jesus was male a crucial point of emphasis for men. 'If Jesus is to have any meaning for men, we must affirm his maleness as a significant part of his humanity, while acknowledging that his humanity remains the important factor. We perhaps need to emphasize more the fact that Jesus was a man, as well as being God.'[50] How these latter two sentences might read if begun with, 'If Jesus is to have any meaning for women', is one way of evaluating the impact of emphasizing Jesus as a man, and by inference therefore not a woman, for contemporary spirituality, and this will be explored further in Chapter 5.

Further, when female-associated terms and effeminate allusions are used derogatively of men failing to live up to mature Christian manhood – they are sissified, feminized,[51] wimps, nerds, softies[52] – in contrast to Christlike masculinity or godliness, this subtly reinforces the notion that godly behaviour is somehow essentially masculine. 'Certainly, godly character should inform and shape the expression of a man's masculinity; but the development of godly character should not be addressed in such a way that it can easily be construed as a particularly masculine enterprise.'[53]

This emphasis on the *maleness* of Jesus, to which men might relate, is not new but has been the founding basis for patriarchal order in church, home and society for centuries. Whether deliberate or not, the effect of this conflation of masculinity with divinity, while intended to affirm Christian men, does so at the expense of women, which is typical of a patriarchal paradigm.

In many ways, whatever the felt need that it is addressing, this new masculinity is not radically different to its patriarchal forebears. While it in some ways enhances the human experience for men, encouraging their personal development, it perpetuates gender divisions and structures that continue to constrain women.

Understanding Equality

Equality between women and men, along with equality between persons of different age, race, sexual orientation, religion and belief, gender identity, and between persons with a disability and without, is now part of British legislation in terms of negative or anti-discrimination statutes (that outlaw discriminatory practices and enable redress once discrimination has occurred) and in terms of positive duties (that place public bodies under statutory obligation to promote equality regardless of a complaint about discrimination).[54] Legislative measures are both a response to campaigning and attitudinal shifts and the means whereby cultural and social norms are challenged and changed.

Given the development of negative and positive equality duties and their wide application, equality is frequently associated with legislative measures. However, equality is more than about laws, policies and regulations, and about more than equality of opportunity,[55] which is the most common approach used in the UK. In a broader or philosophical and, indeed, theological sense, equality is a profoundly relational concept and 'refers to relationships that empower groups of people who have been considered unequal on the basis of differences, such as race, gender, and class'.[56] This perhaps explains why, to some, equality as achievement or aspiration is welcome as they experience empowerment, while for others, equality is a difficult idea or experience because it involves loss of privilege. The trouble with privilege is that often it is in the nature of a privileged position not to be able to appreciate the advantages of it. Hence, tasting a more so-called 'level playing field' may feel more like discrimination than it does about losing unfair advantage. And sometimes, of course, there is an inequality within a privileged group in terms of the rewards of belonging to that particular group and, therefore, it may be harder to recognize or accept the needs of others outside of the group. Perhaps it is in the nature of a competitive model of relating that we encounter such dynamics.

There is much to be gained by men in pursuing a more equal relationship with women. Women's access to employment, especially when accompanied by equal pay, means that the responsibilities of financial provision for families can be shared. Family-friendly policies in workplaces (parental leave, flexible working, child care provision) serve the interests of fathers as well as mothers and can enable men to have more time with their children and be available to them in times of particular need. Shared domestic and parenting responsibilities offer fathers involvement in their children's lives and relationships not available to previous generations. Having the benefit of women's gifts and abilities in churches and workplaces can not only bring contributions that may be missing (because the women have been absent) but also enable the personal growth and development of everyone involved. The presence of women potentially can change operational dynamics and modes of relating, challenge assumptions, and foster greater inclusiveness.

These are all potential gains. However, a truth about equality is that loss of privilege is still loss. And it involves change. The adjustments required to actualize equality are more welcomed by some than others. Some married men will prefer to have someone else do the domestic chores needed to sustain them in their perceived self-sufficiency. Some men will maintain the privilege of economic power and some will not want the daily work of bringing up children. While frequently it is personal behaviour that must change, so must society's attitudes and institutions that still are not overtly child- and care-friendly. The difficulties of combining work and caring responsibilities that many women experience are not necessarily eradicated by more equality in personal relationships but often come to be experienced also by men. For example, men have concerns that flexible working would mark them out as not committed to their jobs or negatively affect their chances of promotion.[57]

In all these adjustments, whether accepted or resisted, any sense of loss that may go alongside considerable potential gain is loss of power, but it is not victimization. The idea that, because the religious environment is now so feminized and squeezing men out, there is a need for men's groups in churches is a denial of the control that men have had of belief and believers throughout church history and in many ways still retain. Similarly, while anxieties about identity and vexations of self-discovery bound up in the crisis in masculinity resulting from so-called feminization are real and deserve attention, there is a difference between such spiritual malaise and oppression. 'Malaise and oppression are both painful, but they are not comparable.'[58] Safe male-only spaces where men are enabled to explore the dynamics of changing social relations with women may be valuable as part of the process of leaving patriarchy behind. Men-only spaces carved out by definition in separation from women in defence of male privilege (cultural or structural) serve to perpetuate a gender hierarchy known throughout Christendom, albeit adapted to modern sensibilities.

The language of equality is not a first language for theology or more specifically theological anthropology; Christian understanding of human beings and how they relate to one another is expressed in language of human personhood created in the image of God more than it is through modern sensibilities of equality. Equality is not irrelevant, but it has a derivative value. Hence, for Christians, the equality that human beings have with each other comes from their commonality in being creatures of the one Creator. The dignity of each human person comes from our being made in the image of God. Similarly, the inalienable rights that human beings possess without distinction,[59] for Christians, are rooted in the understanding of God as Creator who bestows innate worth on humanity.

The spiritual equality of women and men is no longer an issue in Christian understanding.[60] It is mainstream theological orthodoxy that women and men as women and men are created, loved and redeemed by God without distinction in terms of divine grace bestowed upon them. How women and men function in human society as material beings, however, is another matter and one on which there is disagreement. For some, distinctions of role and function on the grounds of sex are part of the created natural order. For others, while as sexed beings gender may influence a person's role and function, it does not determine it by default.

A feminist argument is that, while gender is not unrelated to biological distinction and indeed (our) material embodiment is affirmed, the notion of difference drawn from such distinction is a social category rather than an ontological or self-evident one. In other words, human society creates and moulds the significance assigned to human gender and this should not be used to subordinate, oppress or discriminate against women. Put simply, difference is what we make it.

A theological argument is that spiritual equality between women and men finds expression in material embodiment. While imperfect in its outworking, it refutes the spiritually equal yet materially differentiated argument that maintains male privilege. Instead, drawing on the life of Jesus and the practice of the first churches, it finds theological resonance with the modern sensibility of equality, even if not wanting to make equality the sole paradigm for how women and men relate together.

5.

Women, Men and Theological Imaginings

The American sitcom *According to Jim* focuses around the family life of Jim, a 'macho everyman' with 'boyish bravado'. In one episode, Jim meets his brother-in-law's new girlfriend, Alicia, and their conversational banter includes the following exchange:

Jim: 'Do you believe in God?'
Alicia: 'Of course, I believe in her.'
Jim: 'God is not a girl.'
Alicia: 'How do you know?'
Jim: 'Because God is a boy's name.'

The idea that 'God is a boy's name' or that 'God is a word for boys',[1] that the Bible is 'more of a story for boys' than girls,[2] or that to represent Christ a person must be male, all speak of how our being female and male is inextricably bound up in what our Christian faith looks and *feels* like. If it was not, there would be no fuss around referring to God as 'she' and to speak of God as 'her' would be unremarkable.

How do we imagine God as women and men? By imagine, I do not mean conjure up out of nothing or that God can mean anything we want. And I do not mean that we should not seek to come to an understanding of God that is grounded in our experiences of faith, Christian communities (both past and present), and wrestling with biblical texts. Rather, Christian imagination is about how we make sense of and grasp the transcendent reality of God involved in the world and our lives. It is how we as creatures come to understand and relate to our Creator. I use the term imagination as a reminder that we do indeed, as expressed by Paul, 'see in a mirror, dimly' and 'know only in part'.[3]

Key in Christian imagination is the idea that humanity is made in the image of God. Related to this is the claim that the incarnate Christ in the person of Jesus is God's unique self-disclosure. This chapter explores both these foundational notions specifically for the meanings they generate for and about women and men.

In Whose Image?

We say we are made in the image of God and yet the chief use we make of humanity as that image to picture God is male. It is not female, nor is it female and male. Even in using impersonal pictures such as rock, fortress, shield, light and shade,[4] God remains overwhelmingly 'he'. God is 'he' to such an extent that, while we claim God has no gender, for many, God as 'she' feels not simply odd but somehow wrong, even dangerously wrong.

When we think of God we begin from that which we know – ourselves and our world. We can do it no other way, because we cannot step outside of ourselves away from the reality of being embodied beings. 'The body . . . is the ground of our subjectivity and the medium of all our experiences. All our knowledge is rooted in our corporeality.'[5] This includes the embodiment of being women and men. What is going on, therefore, when we ignore female persons in our imaging of God?

When in 1973 Mary Daly wrote, 'if God is male, then the male is God',[6] she was encapsulating the dynamic wherein male imagery for God perpetuates inequality between women and men and specifically male dominance over women. While it may be said that of course God is not male and that male language is merely a vehicle for speaking of God, the ubiquitous theology and practice of privileging male references for God (and the accompanying opposition to the inclusion of female ones) tells a different story. It imprints in personal and community understanding an association of God with maleness and a disassociation with femaleness.

Gender-exclusive language is not inclusive. When speaking of human beings, 'man', 'he' and 'his' do not mean 'woman', 'she' and 'hers'. Even when 'man' is used as the generic person, that person is assumed to be male. Hence, to say 'man is the only primate that commits rape' makes sense in a way that 'man being a mammal breastfeeds his young' or 'man has difficulties in giving birth' do not.[7] In our thought systems and in our guts, the generic human person is male, as demonstrated through the following statement: 'When the first ancestor of the human race descended from the trees, she had not yet developed the mighty brain that was to distinguish her so sharply from other species.'[8] The clash between word and image readers experience here exposes the marginalization of women not only from our language but also from our understanding. Gender-exclusive language for human beings contributes to:

> ensuring that in the thought and reality of our society it is the males who become the foreground while females become the blurred and often indecipherable background. *He/man* makes males linguistically visible and females linguistically invisible. It promotes male imagery in everyday life at the expense of female imagery so that it seems reasonable to assume the world is male until proven otherwise. It reinforces the belief of the dominant group, that they, males, are the universal, the central, important category so that even those who are not members of the dominant group learn to accept this reality. It predisposes us to see more male in the world we inhabit.[9]

This shapes our understanding of reality for both women and men, although we experience this reality differently. While men may take their presence, inclusion, value and agency for granted, women have to work out if and how they are present, included, affirmed and able to act. What is more, as Dale Spender points out, it 'is not just that women do not see themselves encompassed in the symbol *he/man*: men do not see them either'.[10] So it is also with our language for God.

The Dominance of Male God-Talk[11]

Our language for God is overwhelmingly male. Male imagery and terminology are dominant in Scripture, creeds, liturgies, sermons, prayers, Christian literature, Sunday schools, Bible study groups, churches, theological academies and everyday conversations. The occasional use of female imagery for God underscores that male terminology is the norm. So, too, do reactions of protest and even revulsion when God is talked of in female terms, which is seen as an aberration. Hence, while Christian confession is that God *created* female and male but is not in Godself female and male, in practice a different understanding pervades our consciousness and practice. 'While officially it is rightly and consistently said that God is spirit and so beyond identification with either male or female sex, yet the daily language of preaching, worship, catechesis, and instruction conveys a different message: God is male, or at least more like a man than a woman, or at least more fittingly addressed as male than as female.'[12]

This embedded, default male terminology has consequences for the way we live together as women and men in church and society. For if God must chiefly be spoken of in male language – or put another way, if femaleness is unfit to speak of God – then men stand in a different relationship to God than do women, and there is a difference in the social standing women and men have relative to each other. A God–man–woman hierarchy results in which men become the mediators between women and God, and men rule over women with divine authority. While in contemporary society that rule may be described as leadership, the structural and conceptual hierarchy remains.

We know that women and men are creatures, not Creator. But as female and male persons we inhabit this distinction between human and divine differently. The near-exclusive use of male language and imagery for God means that, however unconsciously, men's fundamental standing in relation to God is one of 'like me', whereas women's is one of 'not like me'. Given our gendered spheres of life, and our construction of identity not simply in relationship to but in *opposition* to each other as women and men, how could the relationship to God imaged through male metaphors be any other way?

The different positioning of women and men in terms of identification with God has an impact. Since men 'have grown up hearing God called "he" just as they are called "he," they have been affirmed on a profound level over many years.'[13] This contrasts with women's experience:

As a woman brought up in the Christian tradition, I have never heard God described in my image. I have often wondered what it would be like to hear God described habitually in female language. The difference between male and female self-esteem and self-acceptance might in part arise in response to an androcentric understanding of God. What self-confidence must come about from internalizing a message which equates one's self with God![14]

Internalizing either affirmation, value and confidence or a sense of inferiority, unworthiness or self-doubt affects not only individual men and women. Gender relations in society and church reflect these internalizations. Patriarchy is maintained by beliefs in the rightness of male rule, which is given divine endorsement through exclusively male language for God. After all, femaleness has not been left out of our God-talk by oversight or accident. Rather, it has been deliberately excluded as unfit and incapable of being imaginatively used to express the divine. The reasons for this are rooted in dualistic thought, which makes a distinction between God and humanity, between spirit and matter, seeing these as mutually exclusive opposites, in hierarchical relationship, with the former terms being deemed as superior and of greater value than the latter. This framework for understanding the world has influenced both Western philosophical thinking and Christian theology. Maleness and femaleness have been aligned to the basic dualism of God–spirit and humanity–matter. Hence, men were associated with the divine, that which is spiritual, rational, and active, while women were viewed as belonging to the material, that which is natural, emotional and passive, and consequently not considered suitable vehicles with which to speak of God.

> In this profoundly dualistic world view, male is to female as autonomy is to dependence, as strength is to weakness, as fullness is to emptiness, as dynamism is to stasis, as good is to evil. Since the divine principle is pure act and goodness, it necessarily must exclude all dependency, potency, passivity and prime matter. The logic of this set-up leads inexorably to the conviction that the divine can properly be spoken of only on the model of the spiritually masculine to the exclusion of the passive, material feminine.[15]

So pervasive is the male imagery for God, that even those things in dualistic and gendered thinking that are associated with female-ness (whether it is appropriate to do so or not) have been grafted onto the understanding of a male God. As noted in Chapter 4, with the movement for women's social equality challenging the notion of male authority in gender relations, patriarchal language ceased to use the increasingly unacceptable terms of male dominance and female subordination. These were replaced by terms such as (servant) leadership and submission respectively to describe what were said to be natural and God-given gender roles. Similarly, the term hierarchy was replaced by the language of complementarity to soften, while at the same time maintaining, a gender distinction in which men retained functions of leadership and authority. In a parallel and interconnected move, God depicted as author-itative and distant ruler who primarily required obedience was, in modern parlance, reinvented as a compassionate and caring, loving Father. God now had a father's heart. Not a mother's heart. Despite dualistic gender relations identifying care and nurture as feminine qualities, these became characteristics of the male God. In turn they became co-opted into male leadership qualities, sometimes expressed as men being able to own feminine quali-ties in themselves. There is, however, no parallel encouragement of women to own so-called masculine qualities of leadership, authority, autonomy and power.

The male caring deity has often found ready response in women to the extent, as also noted in Chapter 4, that men are said to be finding churches too feminized for their liking. The rediscovery of a male spirituality that engages with the powerful, male, warrior God, for example, is an attempt to make Christianity accessible to men. However, rather than men's alienation being created by women, it has come about by the continuation of patriarchy's attempts to maintain itself by adapting to contemporary sensibilities. Patriarchy requires a male identity based on separation from and power over women. In one of its contemporary forms, the authoritarianism of men and God was softened, although not dismantled, by using the language of complementarity and a loving, kind and caring God. With the resulting culture experienced as too feminized for men in a dualistic gender construction, a particular masculinity is being reasserted now through war-like images.

Exclusive male God-language gives affirmation to men at the expense of women. Hence, how we imagine God is not solely about personal preference. Regardless of whether individual women are comfortable with exclusively male terminology for God ('It doesn't bother me', 'It's not an issue for me', 'I don't mind, really'), its dominance continues to structure gender relations and has a profound impact on all our lives.

Challenging the dominance of male God imagery, however, can be very threatening. Women and men have both internalized self-understandings formed on the basis of being situated primarily 'un-like' or 'like' God. Consider the reaction to the broadcasting of *Jerry Springer: The Opera*, which was met by protests from some Christians about how offensive to God it was. Defence of truth has long been part of the construction of masculinity. Is it possible that, in addition, men's identification with deity means that instances of public disrespecting or insulting God may be taken more personally? That attacks upon God are felt at a deep, albeit unconscious, psychic level as attacks on men themselves? That male dignity is bound up in proper dignity and respect for deity? That patriarchy (and both women and men who support it) takes to heart and finds it of personal slight when God is reviled in these ways? Leaving aside that such protests missed the point of the social satire of this form of musical theatre, which, in this case, was about the diminishment of God's creatures through our hunger for amusement in the debasement of other human beings, the question remains, whom are people really defending?

We can only imagine God through what we know. But if we forget that any particular description of God is a metaphor,[16] that is, an imaginative rather than literal form of speech, the danger is that the image becomes equated with the divine itself and not simply pointing to the divine. We know that it is possible for material objects, such as statues, to be seen this way, but so can ideas and concepts, such as God as king or father: 'refusing to examine our engraved speech leads to an idolatry more sophisticated but no less culpable than that with the golden calf'.[17] A metaphor for God is more likely to become idolatrous if it is used habitually, singularly or dominantly, with the familiar and near-exclusive usage eroding our awareness of its figurative nature. This is no less so when male imagery and language dominate in references to God. Brian Wren has named the dominant male 'metaphor system of divine kingship', KINGAFAP – King-God-Almighty-Father-Protector, as the themes of protection, fatherliness, kingship and omnipotence are frequently presented together in Christian worship and creeds.[18] While an image capable of providing a sense of comfort and security, God as a powerful male monarch has also been used as endorsement to wage war on nations and enforce male power and privilege over women.

It is here that a post-Christendom awareness that intentionally interrogates Christian uses of power has much to offer. It was precisely because God was their king that the Israelites were not to emulate human kingship through crowning a monarch or having a centralized power system. As noted in Chapter 2, Jesus spoke much of the kingdom of God, but it was a kingdom where the outcasts, powerless and insignificant were welcome and in which the greatest within it was not a tyrannical ruler but a servant of all. Its 'king' rode humbly on a donkey, refused to meet violence with violence, and was crucified. This use of the metaphor of kingdom maintains God's transcendence but does not involve hierarchical dominance that subordinates one sex, race or group of people to another. It was a deliberate deployment of a metaphor, along with that of God as father, which contrasted with the autocratic and hierarchical system of the Roman Empire and its emperor. It was refreshingly liberating for those who first heard it, living under Roman rule, and has the possibility of speaking profoundly to us today, if we can find our way to experience the surprise of its message.

Even a post-Christendom hermeneutics, however, is faced with searching questions as we seek to interrogate gender power relations. If the incarnate Christ, in the person of Jesus, is God's ultimate self-disclosure, how significant is the fact that Jesus was male? And what do we take from Christ's submission to the violence of the cross into how we relate as women and men? I address each of these questions in turn.

Male as God Incarnate?

What meaning are we to take from the fact that Jesus was male? From the Middle Ages, it has been argued that Christian priests must be male in order to represent Christ to the people; to be male as Christ was a male. It has not been argued that priests must also be Jewish, freeborn, living under foreign occupation, Palestinian and in their early thirties. Whatever meaning may be found in each of these characteristics for the particular time in history of the incarnation, none has been used as being a necessary criterion for candidates for ordination. Being male, however, has.

The maleness of Jesus has not, of course, been the only argument used against women as priests or their carrying out the offices or functions of leadership. Or put another way, it is not necessary to defend women's exclusion from leadership by appealing to the fact that Jesus was male. Others point to what is said to be Jesus' practice of only appointing men, and in particular the twelve apostles, and to church tradition, which is said to have followed this pattern. These arguments join with ideas about natural or God-given gender complementarity and convictions that Scripture teaches that God has so ordained leadership as male. The picture of which argument is used in which ecclesial context is complex; different understandings of priesthood require different or perhaps overlapping justifications for excluding women.

However, arguments about priesthood, although connected, are not my concern here. This is not because they are not important in and of themselves, and nor is it because the episcopal hierarchies of both Catholic and Anglican traditions contrast with ecclesial patterns evident within Anabaptism. I want to ask a more fundamental question about what meaning we take from Jesus' maleness. While arguments about priesthood – its meaning, nature and composition – make various use of Jesus as a man, these arguments both reflect and perpetuate ideas about the relative status of femaleness and maleness in relation to deity, which in turn impact on the relationship between women and men. And that is the focus here.

So, what does the fact that God incarnate as Jesus was male say about women and men? Does it, in fact, say anything at all? Or has it become a patriarchal weapon to maintain power over women by the implication that maleness is an essential characteristic of deity? Or at least, that there is more affinity between maleness and divinity than femaleness and the divine?

Sometimes in pondering the significance of Jesus's sex, the question is posed of whether God could have become incarnate as a woman. I suggest, however, that this is not the relevant question. It may be that in first-century Jewish society under Roman occupation, the social and physical embodiment as a freeborn male of artisan class was a necessary constraint upon divine incarnation. And there may be other reasons that make sense of why the Messiah appears in the person of Jesus. The question that impacts our lives is whether there is anything about women and femaleness that means it is not suitable to image the divine. Is there anything about female personhood and embodiment that means it is incompatible with divine incarnation? For if we say, think, feel or act (despite, perhaps, of what we say we believe) as if femaleness is incompatible with divine incarnation, as if the meta-phor 'image of God' means something different for women than it does for men, then we do not have equal personhood between women and men. This is not to deny that sexual differentiation exists in human personhood. But it is to argue that sexual differen-tiation cannot be used as reason for different standing of women and men before God.

Both Scripture and history give us examples of people encoun-tering Christ in female form. The New Testament understanding of the church as the body of Christ endorses this correlation between Christ and women and is most graphically illuminated in the record of the conversion experience of a young Pharisee called Saul. Saul had watched approvingly as Stephen had been stoned to death in Jerusalem. In the ensuing persecution that scat-tered the Jerusalem church throughout Judea and Samaria, Saul is described as 'ravaging the church by entering house after house; dragging off both men and women' whom he imprisoned.[19] Saul, with the backing of the chief priests in Jerusalem, sought to continue his intense and vehement persecution of Christians in Damascus. Saul's encounter with the risen Christ on the road as he approached Damascus confronted him with the question, 'Why do you persecute me?' Christ's self-identification is, 'I am Jesus, whom you are persecuting.'[20] To drag Christian *women* off to prison was to persecute Jesus.

In the post-New Testament era, women have also been identi-fied with Jesus. As mentioned in Chapter 2, in the second century,

Blandina hung on a stake in an amphitheatre where 'she seemed to be hanging in the shape of a cross' so that other Christians being beaten and burned 'saw in the form of their sister him who was crucified for them'.[21] More recently, writing of four North American Christian women murdered in El Salvador in 1980 Jon Sobrino commented that the 'murdered Christ is here in the person of four *women*'.[22] Similarly, Chung Hyun Kyung has spoken of recognizing 'the Christ disfigured in his passion' in women who have been dehumanized by oppressive systems.[23]

This idea of encountering Christ in female form through the lives of women does not challenge the historical particularity of Jesus as male. As Elizabeth Johnson states, Jesus' maleness is a constitutive element of his identity, part of his historical contingency; the difficulty arises, rather, with the way Jesus' maleness is constructed in androcentric theology and ecclesiology and it would not 'in a more just church . . . even be an issue'.[24] This male-centred theology and practice have led to the ideological, theological and practical exclusion of femaleness from embodying Christ and symbolizing the divine. And in doing so it has endorsed a male theological and social hierarchy over women. It is this order that is challenged by encounters with Christ in female form because such encounters bear witness to God's presence that does not simply not abhor (in the words of the hymn 'O come, all ye faithful'), but rather finds it fitting to be manifest in female embodiment. This challenge can be explored, and indeed felt deeply and viscerally, through encounters with artistic portrayals of a crucified Christ in female form.

The crucifixion has been the focus of artistic works for centuries – it is an image that continues to captivate painters and sculptors whether or not they are motivated by Christian faith conviction. In 1974, for the United Nations Decade for Women: Equality, Development and Peace (1976–85), the English artist Edwina Sandys created a four-foot-tall bronze sculpture of a slumped female nude wearing a crown of thorns, with arms outstretched depicting the cross. Entitled *Christa*, a decade later during Easter Week it was exhibited at the side of the main altar in the Episcopal Cathedral of St John the Divine in New York City. Situated here, it was the source of much controversy and after eleven days it was removed following protests.

The presiding bishop of the diocese who had supported the display commented on the shock of the statue that had caused him to reflect on theological truths that were often ignored: how the incarnation was the taking on of all humanity, male and female, and that the passion, the suffering of Christ, is shared symbolically by all members of the body of Christ. However according to another churchman of the diocese, while enhancing symbols of Jesus by casting them in different skin colours or ethnic characteristics was not objectionable, the *Christa* went too far by 'totally changing the symbol'.[25]

Both these viewpoints are discussing symbolic representations, not the historical particularity of Jesus. Both see the value of a variety of Christic expressions. But for one, ethnic traits are acceptable in the Christ symbol while sexual variation is not. Similarly, class inculturation – Christ as a poor campesino, for example – is accepted, whereas a female Christ figure is not. Here we see how femaleness is construed as opposite to Christ in a way that ethnicity is not. Women are being told, the symbol of Christ is fundamentally 'not like me'.

Despite this message, the symbolic Christ in female form retains its potency. Another work of art also not created as a specifically religious piece is a bronze sculpture by Almuth Lutkenhaus-Lackey, a German-born Canadian artist. *Crucified Woman* depicts a naked young female in cruciform and was intended to portray human suffering. In 1979 it was displayed beneath the chancel cross in Bloor Street United Church in Toronto during Lent and Eastertide, coinciding with a Good Friday service focused on battered wives. Among the reactions to the sculpture was the shock at seeing the depiction of a woman crucified, which led the minister to comment on the realization of how Christian teaching of the incarnation had implied that to become human was to become male. The artist, who was initially hesitant about the sculpture being displayed in the church, was deeply touched by many women telling her that for the first time they had felt close to Christ, seeing suffering expressed in a female body.[26]

The association of this particular sculpture with suffering became more poignant ten years later after it had been given by the artist to Emmanuel College, Toronto, a United Church of Canada theological college. In 1989, three years after its installation, an unsuccessful male applicant who had wanted to study engineering at the Poly-technique Montreal went into an engineering class there, ordered the males present to leave and then began firing on the females who remained. He shot twenty-seven women in the building, fourteen of whom were killed. Back in Toronto, *Crucified Woman* became the focal point of response to this horror, and every year for the following decade a memorial service was held alongside the sculp-ture, which has come to symbolize this dreadful event.

An artistic expression of Christ in female form that, in contrast to *Christa* and *Crucified Woman*, arose out of Christian Lenten reflection is Margaret Argyle's *Bosnian Christa*. In 1993, in response to the accounts of the rapes carried out on Bosnian women in the ongoing conflict in that region, the English artist crafted a four-foot-high work of mixed textiles she named *Bosnian Christa*. This Christa, 'which would speak about the obscenity of rape clearly and graphically',[27] portrays a crucified female form set against a female vulva. Despite its 'disturbing subject matter and explicit sexual imagery . . . the impact of the work is restful rather than aggressive' and the cross it depicts can be 'understood to be standing guard at the mouth of the vulnerable exposed vulva, quietly repelling the aggressor'.[28] Previously, Margaret Argyle had not used the cross in her work, finding it an overused symbol that had become 'almost meaningless' for her. However, reflecting on her completed work she said, 'This God who understands and shares such suffering speaks through a figure of a woman on a cross . . . the cross now has a meaning for me. It's about a God who is in the world and present wherever anyone suffers. That was an enormous revelation for me. I had never associated God with women and their suffering before.'[29]

Whether or not we find depictions of Christ in female form (either in works of art or in poetry and liturgy)[30] images upon which we might wish to reflect, the visceral reactions that such representations provoke tell us much about the underlying symbolism that structures our theology and our gendered social organization.

For example, some objections to visual representations of a crucified female form concern its nudity. There are strong reac-tions to associating a divine symbol with female sexuality, which has long been considered offensive to divinity. What this reveals, however, is how depictions of Jesus are gendered but not sexual. Jesus' maleness is considered of paramount importance but that maleness – or a naked male on a cross – is not associated with sexuality. The male body has become desexualized while the female body represents sexuality, which in turn is considered antithetical to divinity. Similarly with God the Father, who is gendered without being sexual, whereas God depicted as female is often said to carry sexual nuances that are inappropriate for the Godhead. This is not to say that we should start sexualizing the divine. Rather, this response to divine symbols using female imagery tells us more about ourselves than it does about God. In our imagination and understanding we have transferred humanity's sexuality onto women and away from men, and positioned it as incompatible with divinity. Responsibility for sexuality rests with women. This leaves us wanting in our ability to respond to sexual violence against women, including large-scale, systemic rape deployed as a weapon of war. In Bosnia it is thought that up to as many as sixty thousand women may have experienced the brutality and degradation of sexualized violence between 1992 and 1995.[31] It would be ironic, if it were not tragic, therefore, that a replica of the *Bosnian Christa* that Margaret Argyle made was not allowed to be displayed publicly in one academic theology department since it was viewed as 'an inappropriate depiction of divine suffering'.[32]

The nakedness depicted in some images of Christa has met with feminist concern. This is not because femaleness is considered incompatible with divinity, but because of voyeuristic attitudes (the 'male gaze') towards the female body. Given the context of the sexualization of women, the question is whether cruciform female images hinder rather than help women's wellbeing and may even foster sadistic attitudes towards women.

A common reaction to first encounter with the idea or image of Christ in female form is one of shock and/or offence. Indeed, Margaret Argyle talks of her own disgust at her first sight of a Christa.[33] Yet it is this very shockingness that may offer renewed vitality in the meaning of the cross. The sight of the male Christ crucified is part of our cultural landscape. 'The Christian cross has had Jesus hanging on it for so long that people have become numb to its horror and significance.'[34] The shock of the female image is an invitation to re-engage with the incarnation with 'the accretions of years of theology' removed.[35] With the Word made female flesh we can experience the scandal of divine incarnation which has been made invisible by our overfamiliarity with Jesus as male.

At the most basic level, a female-Christ figure challenges the notion that maleness is normative humanity. It bears witness that God became human. It does not change the historical particularity of Jesus, nor indeed often claim anything other than an identification of God incarnate with the lived realities of women's lives and particularly their suffering. Yet the centrality of a suffering figure in Christianity, whether shown as male or female, is itself played out in our social relations as women and men and in this, too, Christendom has imprinted our theological imaginings.

The Cross, Christendom and Gender Relations

The meaning we take from Christ's suffering on the cross not only has theological ramifications. It also impacts on the social relations between women and men. Indeed, the sense we make of the crucifixion provides theological rationale for how women and men should relate.

Many women and men have found comfort and solidarity in their own suffering in the understanding that God identifies with us and shares our pain through Christ's suffering on the cross. Our God is not remote from, unmoved by, nor indeed inexperienced in, human suffering. We are not alone, we are not forgotten, and we are not abandoned in the travail of human existence.

At the same time, Jesus' submission to the suffering he endured – God did not take this cup away from him[36] – has been used to tell women that they should accept and submit to the suffering and injustice they encounter (not least from male abuse and violence, but also from patriarchal social systems that marginalize and treat women as secondary) rather than to name it as unacceptable and take steps to overcome it. Countless women through the ages have been encouraged or commanded by male priests and leaders that both physical and sexual violence as well as mental cruelty from their husbands is something they should endure as Christ endured his suffering on the cross. Women's own wellbeing has

been secondary to the sacredness of marriage and/or the acceptance of male rule. Nor is this something only of the distant past;
the idea that a woman's discipleship involves an unquestioning
embrace of suffering, without protest, is part of the story of Christianity in our lifetimes and in the contemporary church.[37]

We might think such reasoning that subjects women to continued
abuse at the hands of men stems from a perversion of Christian
theology about the crucifixion of Jesus. But are the roots to be
found closer to mainstream orthodoxy than most of us are aware?
For our understanding of salvation is entangled with ideas about
power, punishment, vengeance, wrath, satisfaction of honour,
and just payment. Key in all this is what meaning we take from
Christ's suffering – what role does it play in the Christian story,
in our story? Did God require suffering and, if so, does suffering
itself become salvific? In other words, did salvation come through
suffering and violence and, if so, is there merit in the suffering
and violence we may experience now and, if so, what about the
violence that men perpetrate against women? While such questions are part of a wide-ranging contemporary debate about the
meaning of Christ's death, here I want to consider the influence
of Christendom on shaping views of atonement, and so we return
to the medieval period when cross and sword were combined to
coerce Christian political and religious allegiance.

The idea of human suffering serving a purpose in our own
salvation was the message given to the Saxons in the Middle
Ages. While Christianity was rooted in Saxony from Roman times,
Carolingian emperors in the eighth and ninth centuries used military might to impose a Catholic orthodoxy on the region as part
of annexing it into the Frankish Empire. Bringing Saxony under
orthodox Christian control, the emperor Charlemagne reasoned,
would lead to their political submission to his empire as members
of Christ's body. Emulating Constantine's innovation of having
cross symbols painted onto military standards which were then
carried into battle,[38] Charlemagne repeatedly waged war against
the Saxons under ornate crosses raised high, claiming divine
power, baptizing those conquered under threat of death. Some
court theologians compared Charlemagne's conversion of the
Saxons to Christ defeating death through his crucifixion, descent
into hell, and resurrection. Clergy appointed by the emperor told

the Saxon people that their defeat and wounds from battle were God's punishment for their pagan sinfulness.

The notion (and indeed experience) of punishment and suffering through military conquest became echoed in eucharistic liturgical understanding and practice. Charlemagne imposed a single eucharistic rite throughout his empire. In contrast to earlier practice which 'made the incarnate, transfigured, risen, and glorified body of the living, eternal Christ present and united the church with the Resurrection', this newer rite 'reenacted the Crucifixion and made the bleeding, dead body of the past, historical Christ present, and united communicants with his suffering and dying'.[39] Jesus was sacrificed daily in the Eucharist, the consecrated elements being the material, historical body of Christ, with the bread and wine making present the crucified body and blood of Christ.[40] This Christ came as judge, and unrepentant sinners who took the Eucharist ate and drank damnation on themselves. Jesus was a victim, yes, but one 'whose power lay in his suffering and its judgment against sinful humanity'.[41]

In the 960s, out of this coercive context of military subjugation, the Saxon Gero Cross was crafted, a life-size oak carving, gilded in gold, depicting a dead Jesus hanging on a cross. It is the earliest surviving crucifix sculpture of a dead Christ and is unprecedented in its depiction of his suffering. This dramatic change in Christian imagination elicited Rita Nakashima Brock and Rebecca Ann Parker's comment, 'It took Jesus a thousand years to die.'[42] Earlier images of Christ on a cross were of Jesus depicted not as dead but as resurrected, as the one who had defeated death. These *Christus Victor* images show Jesus erect and strong, clothed and crowned, with eyes open, rather than stripped and wounded, with body and head sagging and eyes closed; he is not suffering but is alive and reigning from the tree.

Although the idea of Christ as the one who conquers evil and liberates humanity from oppression was fundamental in the pre-Christendom church, the earliest *Christus Victor* images date from the fifth century. Visual representations (as distinct from the Christian practice of signing the cross)[43] appear to be absent before that time. Perhaps unthinkable to a church before Christendom when crucifixion remained an official state penalty (only outlawed by the emperor Constantine), our evidence from the early church is of a Christian imagination fed by images of God's blessing and grace. The Roman catacomb images portray Jesus' birth and baptism, but not his death, nor do they have images related to judgement and hell. Rather, Jesus is shown as shepherd, healer and miracle worker; he raises Lazarus, heals the paralytic, and feeds the people with bread and fish. St Appollinaire Nuova Church in Ravenna, Italy, originally constructed for the Arian military leader Theoderic in the early part of the sixth century, has twenty-six panels telling the story of Jesus.[44] Thirteen tell the story of his passion, beginning with the Last Supper. Simon of Cyrene is shown carrying the cross for Jesus, the next scene is of an angel at the empty tomb and then of Christ resurrected. Again, there is no crucifixion image. 'Christ in the art of the early Church was shown in his human life or sprung to new life – never dead.'[45]

However, by the late ninth century, Carolingian manuscripts used by priests began showing Christ dead on a cross. There followed images of Christ's blood spurting from his side directly into a chalice and, by the eleventh century, 'life-sized images of the Crucifixion appeared in churches throughout northern Europe to remind the faithful of their crime of killing Christ and to teach them fear of God's judgment'.[46] Crucially, the Carolingians 'constructed a Christian piety that used violence to convert pagans and then taught its victims to regard their violation as justified and sanctified'.[47]

At the end of the eleventh century, three years after Pope Urban II initiated the first Crusade in 1095, the Archbishop of Canterbury, Anselm, published his own systematic understanding of salvation. In the context of the feudal system, Anselm saw human offence to God as that of vassals who had failed to give their feudal lord his due – honour, allegiance and obedience. They owed a great debt to God (as many of those who failed to supply what their ruling nobility asked of them owed to their landlords). God requires justice, which must, for his own dignity, involve appropriate payment. Satisfaction is due in order to restore proper order (which is why Anselm's theology is described as the satisfaction theory of atonement). In this case, the only adequate satisfaction is death, but the death of human sinners is insufficient. God becomes human in the person of Christ, his death giving satisfaction enough for all of humanity. God's forgiveness then becomes a just act, because the debt has been paid. While humanity is unable to redeem itself, people could nevertheless express their thanks and gratitude by mirroring Christ's sacrifice. This was a theology essential to fuel the Crusades. 'Killing and being killed imitated the gift of Christ's death, the anguish of his self-sacrifice, and the terror of his judgment.'[48]

While the graphic visual imagery around Christ's death was rejected by Reformation theologians, Anselm's theology was not. However, rather than viewing the rift between God and humanity as one requiring satisfaction because of affront to God's honour, they saw sin as being about breaking God's law. Justice was served by punishment being carried out, and Jesus stands in humanity's place, his death being the penalty exacted. (Hence, this theology is often described as penal substitution.) There is an emphasis on forensic justice – that due process is involved in our salvation, and this judicial resolution involves the price of Christ's death. Hence, God requires this violence, albeit taken upon Godself in the person of Jesus.

Crucial in all of this for our consideration of gender relations is the part that suffering plays in these ideas about salvation. For these views place the death of Christ as central, not his life or even his resurrection. Indeed, Anselm does not even mention Christ's resurrection in his argument – it is not required for his theology of atonement. However removed we are from the detail of these theological formulations of the last thousand years about the meaning of Christ's death, the idea of the necessity of suffering, which in turn can be seen as in some way meritorious and to be commended, is embedded in the traditions of the church(es) that we have inherited. And when combined with scriptural texts interpreted through a patriarchal lens, Christ's servanthood becomes gendered with men emulating a servant leadership, and too often, women being assigned the role of suffering servant.

Not only do women internalize the idea that God sanctions violence against them, but also those who perpetrate the violence find support for their actions in a divine mandate. This support is fed by patriarchal interpretations of selected Scripture, such as: Eve's creation out of Adam making her secondary to him (and hence all women subordinate to men); Eve's responsibility for bringing sin into the world through eating of the forbidden tree (and hence women's general lack of trustworthiness, and even blameworthiness); Paul's words that wives be subject to husbands; and various entreaties that women be silent, without voice or authority. Priests and pastors, on the basis of 1 Peter 3:1–6, have counselled that wifely obedience to an abusive husband may be the cause of his salvation and hence the violence should be endured, and even that wives concentrate on amending their behaviour that is provoking their husbands to maltreat them.[49]

We may want to say that this is an abuse of Scripture and male power, that this is a perversion of the story of the crucifixion, which is about Christ bearing the penalty so we do not have to. After all, plenty of Christians hold to ideas of the death of Jesus being required to satisfy God's justice (rather than, for example, the result of human actions of those unwilling to follow Jesus) without resulting in violent behaviour, although systems and behaviours that continue to marginalize women and subordinate them remain. And certainly violence against women is not simply a religious phenomenon.[50] It is part of patriarchy's toolkit and is a consequence of women's inequality and of male power over women (and not simply an abuse of that power), whether or not religiously endorsed. It is both an outcome of and a means to perpetuate male dominance over women. Indeed, Marjorie Procter-Smith says the 'hard reality of domestic violence puts a face on those often rather vague concepts of sexism, patriarchy, and androcentrism'.[51] However, she also states that the fact that 'domestic violence occurs in the homes of "church-going" Christians, including the homes of Christian clergy, ought to make us wonder what is being heard, seen, said, and done in our Christian assemblies that allows the violence to continue.'[52]

Our theological imaginings have social consequences. We can continue to marginalize, exclude and make invisible women in the way we understand and express faith. We can continue to think, act and speak as if the male is norm, and women are secondary. We can keep feminizing self-sacrifice so that women are socialized or pressured through church traditions into being victims. Or we can, together, as women and men, revisit our theological imaginings as we wrestle to grasp the transcendent reality of God in a world after Christendom.

6.

Gender Relations and the New Testament

Both feminists and Anabaptists talk about reading the Bible with a hermeneutics of suspicion. This means coming to the text alert to the way in which it has been interpreted down the centuries from the point of view of those who have been in positions of power.[1] Those people at the top of various hierarchies of power have determined how the text has been understood and applied; they have been the ones to tell those in subordinate positions what the text means. When Cecil Alexander wrote her children's hymn, 'All things bright and beautiful', published in 1848, it included the verse: 'The rich man in his castle, the poor man at his gate, He made them high or lowly, and ordered their estate.' Usually left out of contemporary renditions, this verse reflected the dominant view of the time that social inequality was ordained by God; the Lord God had indeed 'made them all' in their economic strata.

In terms of gender relations, a hermeneutics of suspicion means coming to the text aware that it has been men, often (if not exclusively) elite, male clergy separated from women, who have interpreted the Bible and told women who to be, what to do and, just as frequently, what *not* to do. From a standpoint of male privilege which has viewed women sometimes as deficient, sometimes as dangerous, but nearly always designated as subordinate, men have told women how they should think, feel and act, justifying this on the basis of biblical teaching. The dominance of patriarchy has meant that often this understanding has been internalized by women; women themselves have seen in the Scriptures a God-ordained order of gender relations that subordinates women to men.

So pervasive has been this view that even those women and men who intuitively know that such teaching is incongruent with their sense of themselves, their experience, and their understanding of God can find it hard to see in Scripture resources that speak of a different way of relating. The weight of centuries of a dominant patriarchal voice mean that other readings have been – and still are – obscured from view.

The task of reading differently – of being alert to the gender power relations embedded in text and in interpretations – is enormous. I concentrate in this chapter on how we might respond to the overwhelming tendency there has been to understand gender relations on the basis of a select number of verses (sometimes referred to as the 'hard passages') in the New Testament.[2] These are taken to encapsulate the way women and men are to be and behave specifically as female and male persons and in relation to one another. These verses are treated as the first and the final words on the matter. The dominant way of understanding these texts has always had something to say about men as well as women, but it has been women who have been constrained by them the most. This is because, dominantly interpreted as endorsing a patriarchal gender order in home, church and public life, men generally have found them supporting rather than challenging their self-understanding and/or lived experience. While exploring the New Testament text for new ways of relating will hold challenges for both women and men, arguably it is the current construction and practice of patriarchal masculinity (including that which is unconscious or unwelcome) that will come under greater scrutiny in this process.

Expansive New Testament Reading

In the light of the contracted use of the New Testament when thinking of gender relations, I suggest three expansive ways of reading the text that are helpful to combine: reading with a wide-angle lens; a panoramic view; and the close-up reading of a telephoto lens.

The first way of reading, from a wide-angle lens, involves taking a broad look at the text when thinking about gender relations. Rather than seeing social relations between women and men expounded only in a few verses, this approach engages with the whole of the text. This is not just about recovering stories of women that are either obvious or more hidden in the text, as valuable as this is (see further below). It also is about uncovering the story of gender in unlikely places, such as I explored in Chapter 2 when thinking about the impact of responding to Jesus' call to follow him in the context of the social and political structures of the time. It means attempting to come to the New Testament without the shadow of centuries of hierarchical interpretations about gender. And it means asking unfamiliar questions of a familiar text.

In this endeavour, the Anabaptist consistent emphasis on Christocentric interpretation has much to offer. Such Jesus-centred interpretation 'means that the Bible, as a record of what God has said and done in many generations, must be viewed through the prism of the revelation of God in Jesus Christ. The Old Testament points forward to him; the New Testament points back to him.'[3] The life, teaching, death and resurrection of Jesus (and not just the latter two) become not only core to understanding the Bible,[4] but also essential for contemporary Christian praxis. If we engage the gospels as accounts of the ministry and mission of Jesus on their own terms rather than filtered through the so-called 'hard passages' of the epistles, we may have different encounters with the text as women and men.

The call to follow Jesus is given to women as it is to men. It is important for women and for men to see women in the gospel accounts. For implicitly, in the same way that 'the male is norm' and the generic human being is male,[5] much Bible reading has made discipleship normatively male. Compounded by the conflation of the twelve (who were male) with all of Jesus' followers (who were many and both female and male), in popular imagination the generic Christian disciple is male. In addition, concentration on select passages in the epistles that specifically focus on the behaviour of Christian women moves the emphasis away from the gospels or, at least, qualifies and defines the outworking of the gospel for women.

Reading with a wide-angle lens means that rather than seeing women defined, 'explained' and shaped by those texts that are said to provide specific instructions about what women cannot do, should do and should be (they cannot teach men; they should not speak in front of men; they must ask their husbands at home; they should be subordinate to men; they must marry, bear children and raise their families; they must obey husbands; they must be silent; they must be of a gentle disposition; they must be modest), women are seen by themselves and by men as engaging with the whole of the text.

For example, what does it mean to be peacemakers – as women, as men, as women and men together? What does it mean to hunger and thirst for righteousness – as women, as men, as women and men together? When Jesus said the greatest commandment was to love God and the second to love our neighbour as ourselves, how do we respond? How do we love our enemies? How do we 'not worry', guard ourselves against 'all kinds of greed' and store up treasure in heaven?[6] Of course, these verses are worked out in our contemporary gendered context, and as such may look different for women and men in different situations. But that in and of itself is not determined by the gospel accounts. So while there may be gendered expressions of our discipleship, the gospel may also challenge our contemporary practice. The import of this can be seen in terms of the demanding ethic to deny the self. If gender relations are structured in a God–man–woman hierarchy, then Jesus' words about self-denial have different consequences for women than for men. However, in the light of Christendom's legacy of the meaning of self-sacrifice and suffering in the lives of women (as discussed in Chapter 5), what does it mean today for women and for men to deny themselves, take up their cross and follow Jesus?[7] What should it *not* mean? And how might we change our structures and culture so that discipleship for women and for men does not involve abuses of power? A broad reading of the Scriptures that is Jesus-centred allows the text to interrogate our own gender practice.

The second expansive way of reading the New Testament is taking a panoramic view. This concerns looking at the early church as we meet it in the New Testament – in the book of Acts that narrates the story of the spread of the gospel and in various letters to localized communities of believers and some individuals. This panoramic view will also take into account the gospels and the book of Revelation, as they were all produced in the context of the first Christian communities. A panoramic view, therefore, bears in mind the diversity of early Christian location, experience and expression in the context of the politics and society of the ancient world.[8]

A panoramic reading of the New Testament sees growth, change (the situations are dynamic not static) and indeed conflict reflected in the story of the early church, which was not immune from the realities of wrestling with what it meant to follow Jesus. The book of Acts recounts in detail (twice – once in telling the story of Peter's experience and a second time when Peter explains what happened to him to the Jewish Christians in Jerusalem when they protested about his behaviour)[9] how Peter came to the realization that the good news was for Gentiles as much as it was for Jews. We know that some prominent Jewish Christians struggled with living out this realization.[10] We know that there was a further difference of opinion among early leaders that led to Paul and Barnabas working separately rather than continuing together.[11] We also know that this particular difference, over the trustworthiness of Mark in the eyes of Paul, was not the end of the story and Mark subsequently joins Paul's company again and is commended by him.[12] We know that there were different leaders who inspired loyalty from different groups of believers.[13] We know of broken relationships among early believers.[14] We know that there were false teachers influencing Christians.[15] We know that some early Christians faced demanding changes in their behaviour.[16] And we know that early Christian communities faced ongoing pressures and challenges in their discipleship and life together.[17]

A panoramic view guards against a false or neat conformity imposed on Christians in the first churches and presents us rather with living, and even 'untidy', bodies of believers. In the same way that we have four gospels providing, initially for different communities of believers, some diversity of expression of the mission and ministry of Jesus, so too the other writings of the New Testament open windows on a variety of Christian churches. As I suggested in Chapter 2, the New Testament epistles contain many voices as part of a conversation about what it means to follow Jesus.[18] This is not to overlook the commonality of the faith that all New Testament writings affirm.[19] Rather, in a panoramic reading we enter into the vibrancy, energy and dilemmas of early

Christian communities and from that vantage point we can ask questions of our own.

Reading with a panoramic lens allows us to see how women and men relate as part of a bigger picture of early church life. The epistles were written, on the whole, to groups of believers and would have been received in communal settings. As with the gospels, it is important for women and for men to see women as part of these early Christian communities: Women and men were called to the one body; women and men were those in whom the word of Christ should be allowed to dwell richly; women and men were those who should teach and admonish one another in all wisdom; women and men had hearts of gratitude in which they sang psalms, hymns and spiritual songs to God; and women and men were to do everything, whether in word or deed, in the name of the Lord Jesus, giving thanks to God through him.[20] Women as well as men were to be imitators of God and live in love, as Christ loved.[21] No wonder, then, that we know from the New Testament that women were active in praying and prophesying, teaching and spreading the gospel, and hosting churches, providing support and acting as benefactors.[22]

The third way of reading the New Testament when thinking about gender relations is, I suggest, using the telephoto lens – a close-up look at particular passages which are most often alluded to in thinking about the relationship between women and men. While I have argued it is misplaced to begin with these verses (or indeed to use them as the primary interpretive filter) when thinking about the social relations of women and men, that does not mean we should ignore them. We need to engage with them because they have been – and continue to be – so influential in Christian imagination. Close-up reading, when carried out alongside wide-angle and panoramic New Testament reading, offers us the opportunity to change our encounter with these texts from that of a fearsome burden reifying women's oppression to that of windows opening onto some of the first Christians' experiences of living out their faith. As with the rest of the New Testament, these verses show us Christians working out what it means to follow Jesus in their particular circumstances, as we likewise endeavour to do in ours.

The first two of these three expansive ways of reading the New Testament are illustrated in Chapter 2. The remainder of this chapter, therefore, shows the third focused reading of the tele-photo lens by looking closely at 1 Timothy 2:8–15.

1 Timothy 2:8–15

The first letter to Timothy is a good passage to use for a close-up reading that is part of an expansive approach to understanding the New Testament. Of all the so-called 'hard passages', while not necessarily considered first, frequently it has been treated as the 'trump card' of biblical witness to the place of women as subordinate to men. Whatever conclusions are drawn from the shared, divinely created humanity of female and male in Genesis 1 – 3, the liberating gender praxis of Jesus contained in the gospels, the astounding demolishing of hierarchies in Galatians 3:28, or the enthusiastic participation of women and men in public worship at the church in Corinth, a few verses in 1 Timothy (2:11–14) are used to settle any dispute or doubts about the relationship of women to men. Women may not teach men, may not have authority over men; women must be silent (and men must speak), women must submit (and men must rule). And why is this so? Because Adam was formed first, then Eve, and it was Eve who was deceived and sinned. In effect, these verses have become the interpretive lens through which all other biblical material has been understood.

As mentioned in Chapter 2, 1 Timothy is thought by some scholars to have been written by an author using Paul's name (and possibly also borrowing Timothy's name for the recipient) rather than being written by Paul himself. Views of non-Pauline authorship tend to date the letter to well after Paul's death and towards the end of the first or beginning of the second century. Consequently, some commentators place less emphasis on its content, seeing it as an expression of a church that (perhaps understandably) has compromised with its surroundings and lost some of the liberating aspects of the gospel with respect to women and men. However, this viewpoint implicitly accepts a reading of the text as the author prohibiting all women from ever teaching, or having authority over, men. What it omits is that alternative readings are possible, indeed more plausible, and that these have substance regardless of the question of authorship.[23] Or put another way, whether or not Paul is accepted as the author, we do not have to accept that the letter advocates a restricted and subordinated place for all women in Christian communities – either then or now.

Ephesus

In revisiting what these verses in 1 Timothy may mean we begin with Ephesus – the place where Timothy was when he received the letter, and where the letter urges him to remain (1 Tim. 1:3). Ephesus was a large, busy and prosperous city on the western coast of Asia Minor. By the New Testament era it was the fourth largest city in the Roman Empire and the most important in the Roman province of Asia. It was the gateway to Asia from Greece and likewise the conduit for oriental culture and tradition to move further westwards. This flow of people brought religious diversity to the city. In addition to the prominence amidst ancient polytheism of the cult of Artemis (see below), in Ephesus magic practices and superstitions flourished; books of incantations and magical formulas were known among ancient Roman and Greek writers as 'Ephesian letters' or writings (*Ephesia grammata*). The imperial cult was in evidence; at least one temple dedicated to Rome and Caesar existed there in the apostle Paul's time. Ephesus also had a large settled Jewish population, possibly as many as seventy-five thousand persons inhabiting around one quarter of the city, who had successfully obtained civil rights in the previous century under Roman rule.

Ephesus was the home of one of the seven wonders of the ancient world – the Artemision, a temple dedicated to Artemis. Artemis was the name of a Greek goddess who, in the context of Asia Minor where the dominant deities were not only female but also maternal, was worshipped as the great mother goddess. Artemis was created first and hence chose for herself a male consort rather than getting married, 'so there was a strong cultural assumption that women were both prior to and independent of men'.[24] Her temple in Ephesus was served by thousands of people, female and male, among whom were both priests (some of whom were castrated males) and priestesses (female virgins). Artemis was viewed as the goddess of hope for women; she protected women in child-bearing. Inscriptions refer to her as 'Artemis the Great' and she was worshipped throughout Asia and far beyond (Acts 19:27). Each year for one month the city ceased its work and devoted itself to the Artemis cult; there were games, a festival and special sacrifices in her honour.

Artemis was the city's protector and source of much wealth generation. Foreign kings were among those who deposited their money in the Artemision for safe-keeping given its sacred and inviolable status. The temple in turn made loans using this money, making it the largest bank in Asia. It also received income from visiting pilgrims who flocked to Ephesus to visit the temple and attend festival events. Among those in the city who benefited were the silversmiths who made silver shrines of the goddess. Fears for their own prosperity led a group of them to agitate against Paul whose preaching was drawing people away from worshipping the goddess and visiting her temple.[25] 'Great is Artemis of the Ephesians!' was the rallying cry of the crowd as they forcibly got hold of two of Paul's travelling companions, Gaius and Aristarchus, and dragged them off to the theatre in Ephesus that is estimated to have been able to seat some twenty-five thousand people, and where they continued to chant their adoration to the goddess, according to Acts, for two more hours.[26]

Paul spent a protracted period of time in Ephesus. After his initial visit, he returned and spent more than two years there proclaiming the gospel, debating with Jews and Greeks (Acts 19:8–10). It was a place of healing from sicknesses and evil spirits (Acts 19:11–17). Many new believers gave up their magic practices, and publically burned their pagan religious books valued at fifty thousand silver coins (Acts 19:18–19). For Paul it was also a place of struggle that he characterized as fighting with wild animals (1 Cor. 15:32) and where there were many adversaries (1 Cor. 16:8–9).

The Church in Ephesus

The church at Ephesus struggled with the influence of false teachers. They were teaching different doctrine (1 Tim. 1:3) and were caught up with myths and speculative lengthy genealogies (1 Tim. 1:4). Some wanted to be teachers of the (Jewish) law but had no understanding of what they were talking about (1 Tim. 1:7). Paul had warned the Ephesian church elders that this would happen, that some from among them would distort the truth (Acts 21:29–30). He was well aware of the need for the church at Ephesus to have a good grounding in Christian understanding. Indeed, Paul had not only proclaimed the gospel in Ephesus but had also spent time teaching new believers whose new-found faith had not heard of the Holy Spirit (Acts 19:1–7). An eloquent and passionate Jewish Christian from Alexandria, Apollos, came to Ephesus and he too needed some further instruction on the Way of God as revealed in and through Jesus. This he received from Paul's friends, Priscilla and Aquila, and was able to powerfully contend with the Jews over their Scriptures when he continued his ministry in Achaia (Acts 18:24–8). The fact that both Priscilla and her husband took Apollos aside and 'explained the way of God to him more accurately' (Acts 18:26) tells us that even if 1 Timothy 2:12 is understood as an instruction against women teaching men, it cannot be a universal proscription. Luke is adamant that the evidence is that Priscilla's instruction of Apollos in Ephesus was beneficial for the gospel and he includes it as part of his carefully investigated and orderly account of the activities of the apostles (Acts 1:1; Luke 1:1–4).

False teaching was not the only problem facing the emerging church in Ephesus. There were tensions over money and power as well – and the power and spiritual gain that money might procure. The wealthy are to be commanded not to seek material or social reward in this life on account of their riches (1 Tim. 6:17–20). Instead they are to 'do good, to be rich in good works, generous, and ready to share' (1 Tim. 6:18). These verses are a criticism of the patronage system (see Chapter 7) whereby people who provided some form of benefice either in terms of money or connections were rewarded with the loyalty and obligation of others to whom they lent their patronage. 'In other words, the author, in a reasonable way, is saying to the rich that they are not to expect, because of their gifts and good works in the community, the submission of the members or the leaders. They should not expect to be given honor, recognition, or praise, as they were accustomed to receive in the meritocratic Greco-Roman society.'[27] It is in this letter that we have the often misquoted phrase, 'the love of money is a root of all kinds of evil',[28] and the sober reality that a number of those aspiring riches in the Ephesian church had fallen away because of their desire for wealth and earthly prosperity (1 Tim. 6:10). This love of money seems also to have corrupted some Christians' understanding of the gospel; they see godliness in terms of personal gain (1 Tim. 6:5).

So, matters of money, godliness and teaching are intertwined in these struggles for influence and prestige in the church. As we shall see, these themes that appear throughout the letter are not unrelated to the exhortation to women in Chapter 2 – women who had the personal resources consisting of gold, pearls and expensive clothing (1 Tim. 2:9), the attire of the wealthy.

Given the various religious influences in Ephesus it is not surprising there was some syncretism or borrowing of religious words and practices that were thought powerful among various religious adherents. Some itinerant Jewish exorcists invoked the name of Jesus in an effort to emulate what they had seen Paul do, although this resulted in failed and disturbing outcomes (Acts 19:11–16). Paul writes to Timothy of those who have suffered 'shipwreck in the faith' whom he has 'turned over to Satan' (1 Tim. 1:19–20). This may be an allusion to church discipline (for he has done this in order that they may learn not to blaspheme), but the idea of Satan as an instructor may also indicate that in addition to Judaizers influencing the Ephesian Christians, there were gnostic influences at work. While the church in the second century struggled with a more developed Gnosticism,[29] ideas found among its various sects are evident in nascent form in the preceding century. All three pastoral epistles have concerns about false teachers that ring true of gnostic ideas: myths, endless genealogies and speculations; meaningless talk and contradictions in what is taught; wrangling over words; stupid and senseless controversies; and falsehoods about resurrection (1 Tim. 1:4–6, 6:20; 2 Tim. 2:14,16,18,23; Titus 3:9). The final exhortation to Timothy in the first letter is that he avoid the profane chatter and contradictions of what is falsely called knowledge or *gnōsis* from which the term Gnosticism is derived (1 Tim. 6:20). Gnosticism viewed the created world as evil, from which people needed special knowledge (much of which made no sense) to escape. Similar to many mystery rites in ancient religions, this secret or esoteric knowledge was not about a set of truths or proclamations, but came about through some kind of initiation. Women, in particular, played a role in passing this knowledge on – both as adherents and as the female characters in gnostic literary accounts.[30] 'Gnosticism turned upside-down the Genesis account of the Creation and Fall, making the snake a hero who leads Adam and Eve away from God's deception, and presenting Eve as the source of life and enlightenment.'[31]

Praying

The pagan converts at Ephesus had a variety of religious experience before becoming Christians. As herald, apostle and teacher of faith and truth to the Gentiles, Paul outlines how women and men should pray now that they are Christians and no longer following a hybrid of other religious practices (1 Tim. 2:7–10). Men are to pray with holy hands uplifted and without anger or argument, and the women are to pray from a disposition of propriety and good works. The verses relating to women have neither subject nor main verb in the Greek text, but are rather linked to those of the preceding phrase (speaking of men's demeanour in prayer). 'The text is literally, "Likewise, the women . . ." The missing grammatical pieces must be supplied from what precedes: "Likewise *I want* the women *in every place to pray*." '[32] As with other churches, the Christian community at Ephesus consisted of assemblies where the women participated in prayer.

The appropriate deportment[33] that women are to be urged to adopt may touch on a number of scenarios. The need for modest and decent attire seems to reflect the cultural onus on respectable women to behave with decorum in their religious activity (as in the rest of life), which would include an emphasis on a wife's fidelity to her husband. There may also be an allusion to female prostitution. The criticism of ostentatious displays of gold, pearls and expensive clothes suggests that women of some economic standing are in mind, women who may have been among the benefactors of the church who the letter warns should not expect worldly recognition of their patronage, and among those commanded not to be haughty (1 Tim. 6:17). Behaviour deemed inappropriate for women was often characterized as sexual impropriety in the ancient world and so there could be a conflation of these factors.

Learning

Following these words about the nature of women's demeanour in prayer are words often read as a restriction on women. They are, rather, a permissive instruction: 'Let a woman learn' (1 Tim. 2:11), or, 'as a present permissive imperative implies continuous action: let a woman continue learning'.[34] In the context of much false teaching, women were among those who were attracted to (1 Tim. 5:15; see also 2 Tim. 3:6–7) and perhaps even those who spread the falsehoods (1 Tim. 5:13 – the word translated here as busybodies is used for those who practised magic in Acts 19:19). Some younger women in particular had already turned away to follow Satan (1 Tim. 5:15) and the author urges them to 'marry, bear children, and manage their households, so as to give the adversary no occasion to revile us' (1 Tim. 4:14). If the false teaching the letter is concerned to refute included renouncing the world and bodily realities because these were considered inherently evil, exhortation to marriage, children and the life of a household, all in the context of Christian community, may be an affirmation of embodied existence rather than a rejection of it.[35]

In this context of a Christian community finding itself beset by falsehood, the women are endorsed as learners, and this learning is best done not in absolute silence, but with an attitude of calmness and self-control – the author uses the Greek word *hēsychia* (1 Tim. 2:11). The adjectival form of the same Greek word is used just a few verses earlier in 1 Timothy 2:2 to refer to a 'quiet and peaceable' life and in 1 Peter 3:4 of the inner self that has a 'gentle and quiet' spirit. The word for being silent (the verb, *sigaō*), which Paul uses in 1 Corinthians to indicate when speakers in tongues and prophets should restrain themselves so that corporate worship was edifying rather than chaotic and confusing, is not used here in 1 Timothy 2:11.[36] Not only is this learning to be done in a calm and controlled manner, it is to be done in 'full submission'. 'The phrase *silence and submission* is a Near Eastern formula implying willingness to heed and obey instruction.'[37] The submission is therefore either to those who teach or to what is taught, or possibly a reference to the self-control of the learner. There is no suggestion that women are to submit to all men as men, although that has sometimes been assumed because of the verse that follows.

Certainly verse 12, 'I permit no woman to teach or to have authority over a man; she is to keep silent', is connected (grammatically) with verse 11 and its thought therefore is somehow related. The understanding of this verse, in part, rests on the meaning of the Greek word *authentein* – often translated 'to have authority', but which appears nowhere else in the New Testament or in the Septuagint (the Greek translation of the Old Testament), against which to assess its nuance.[38] For in other ancient literature *authentein* often carried negative connotations of usurping authority or domineering, of holding absolute sway. Its related noun meant murderer or perpetrator of an act. Early Arabic versions translated from Greek, Syriac and Coptic sources use words with similar meaning – 'to plot; to be domineering; to act as "lord and master"; to be imperious . . . to be insolent'.[39] The thought in the verse, therefore, that the author does not permit a woman to teach and to domineer can be joined together to mean that a woman should not teach in a domineering manner towards men. Rather, women are to be – again – not silent, but in quietness, the same demeanour (and the same word used: *hēsychia*) as they are to have as learners in the preceding verse. Ian Paul suggests a paraphrase of verses 11 and 12 to capture Paul's intent: 'I won't put up with any of you women setting yourselves upon your own authority and leading people away from the apostolic teaching. Instead, you should take your place along with everyone else as full members of the community of disciples, learning and growing in your faith.'[40]

These verses cannot mean that women are never to teach, nor even never to teach men. As well as Priscilla's work in instructing Apollos in Corinth, Timothy himself had been taught the Scriptures from childhood by his believing mother and grandmother (Acts 16:1; 2 Tim. 1:5; 3:14,15). Paul also sees the value of older women teaching younger women (Titus 2:1–5). He encourages women to prophesy in the Corinthian church (1 Cor. 11:5), with prophecy clearly being understood for the building up, learning and encouragement of the gathered Christian community (1 Cor. 14:26,29–31). In Jesus' own ministry, women were involved in passing on the good news to men (John 4:39; Luke 24:10). In Luke's gospel, it is from Mary's lips that we are given the Magnificat, and in so doing Luke 'indirectly presents her as a teacher of theology, ethics and social justice'.[41]

All of this speaks against understanding 1 Timothy 2:11–12 as a universal prohibition against women teaching. It is rather something required because of the situation in Ephesus (and indeed, arguably, applicable whenever anyone, female or male, twists the gospel). It also means that verse 14, which states that it was Eve who was deceived and not Adam, cannot be understood as indicating that women, because they were women, were prone to deception. Rather, the instruction here concerns the need of the Ephesian church where the author's overwhelming concern is with teaching that accurately reflects the gospel and not distorted understandings influenced by other religious practices and ideas. As R.T. France comments, if Paul 'intended to say that no woman may ever be in a position where she has authority over a man, he has chosen an unnecessarily obscure way to say it!'[42]

While Richard Clark Kroeger and Catherine Clark Kroeger outline a number of ways that verse 12 may be understood, including that the author is forbidding women from exercising a domineering authority, they offer an alternative interpretation. Based on grammatical and literary considerations, they suggest that *authentein* should be understood as meaning origin (from which is derived the notion of authenticity, the English word taken from *authentein*, and which can give rise to concepts of authority).[43] The verse would thus read: 'I do not allow a woman to teach nor to proclaim herself author of man',[44] this combating false teaching (of Gnosticism[45] and the cult of Artemis, or a syncretism of the two) that said woman was responsible for the creation of man. Understanding the word translated 'silence' as peace or harmony, woman 'is to be in conformity [with the Scriptures]'.[46] Certainly this reading makes good sense of what follows where the author states that Adam was formed first and also was not the one deceived. 'Just as the writer asked that women learn in conformity to the Word of God, he now asks that they express their views in harmony with the revelation of the Scriptures: in this case, that woman did *not* create man nor did Eve bring spiritual illumination to Adam.'[47] Pointing out Eve's transgression does not endorse an idea of womankind's moral deficiency, but gives a corrective to influential mystery beliefs flourishing in Ephesus that were antithetical to the gospel.

Living

The final verse in this section is one of the most difficult of which to make sense. 'Yet she will be saved through childbearing, provided they continue in faith and love and holiness, with modesty' (1 Tim. 2:15, which in the Greek uses the definite article: 'the bearing of children'). It is connected by way of contrast to the previous thought about Eve's transgression, which in tradition is associated with increased trauma in giving birth (Gen. 3:16). One view is that the 'she' refers to Eve who is saved through the birth of Christ. Another view is that Christian women are exhorted to be hopeful in approaching childbirth, a potentially hazardous experience in women's lives; many women died in childbirth and many children in infancy or early childhood.[48] The letter begins with a description of Jesus Christ as our hope (1 Tim. 1:2), which perhaps here is given as a corrective to the counter-claim of Artemis as women's hope through child-bearing. Or it may be that verse 15 is correcting the idea that having children was something that is incompatible with salvation, ideas taught among some Ephesian ascetic religious influences.[49] What it cannot mean is that salvation for women comes not through faith in Christ, but in having children. Redemption remains, for both women and men, a journey of faith, love and holiness.

The idea that these verses give divine sanction to male authority over women has been feeding Christian imagination for centuries, obscuring or silencing and even vilifying other interpretations. Whatever allowances one might suggest for the environments that circumscribed the ability to explore biblical witness differently, a post-Christendom ethos offers new possibilities. Remove the assumptions about a gender hierarchy and we can explore afresh what the evidence suggests.

There is some divergence and uncertainty in what I have outlined above, the distance between our world and the text still veiling to some extent our ability to capture its full sense and feel. However, understanding the text in the context of ancient Ephesus is more plausible than reading it as a universal command that women should not teach or have authority over men. The latter does not fit with the New Testament evidence of the active engagement of Christian women in proclaiming the gospel and in the life of the church. Nor does it do justice to the whole of the text of 1 Timothy, which not only gives us clues to the meaning of these few verses but also gives a picture of a church wrestling with new-found faith in the midst of powerful religious and social forces. Indeed, here I have concentrated on thinking about the text in its original context rather than on our dialogue with the text and the many things it has to contribute to our contemporary situation.[50]

The biblical text resists our attempts to tame it purely for our purposes. To enter into dialogue with it is to experience the ambiguities and struggles of the first generations of Christians as well as our own. As we return again and again to its narratives, we may see fresh stories that enrich and inspire us and compel us forward, even in the midst of things that have previously stunted our growth and held us back. From the Ephesian story we have the surprising words, 'Let a woman learn'. For all the matters that remain for discussion in 1 Timothy, how might it transform the lives of us all if women, along with men, immersed themselves in the deep waters of God's passion for humanity and brought their learning to bear on how Christian faith is understood, practised and inhabited?

7.

Post-Christendom Women
and Men

In 1994, the Catholic Church opened up the possibility of girls serving at the altar during Mass, something previously restricted to boys. At the discretion of each diocesan bishop, permission could now be given for girls as well as boys to assist at the celebration of the Eucharist.[1] A couple of years later, while interviewing Christian women for my doctoral research, several interviewees spoke about this recent development. One woman considered that there were now female altar servers 'only because they couldn't get the boys to keep going, you know, so they've actually said, well, we'll have to broaden it out'. Not so, according to another Catholic woman. She thought it was allowing girls to be altar servers that was resulting in a reluctance of boys to fulfil this function 'because they think it's too sissy now to be on the altar'.[2]

While these explanations seem contradictory, they are not mutually exclusive but reflect a particular gender dynamic in which individual altar girls and boys are caught up. Both explanations present a picture of masculinity that is constructed in opposition to femaleness. This masculinity is safeguarded either by the exclusion of women from various functions or by women's admission because of the withdrawal of men from those same spheres. This model of female exclusion rather than that of partnership or mutual co-operation belongs to an ethos that subordinates female personhood in order to protect male identity.

An adult example comes from the debate within the Church of England about appointing women as bishops for the first time. Included in the church's process were draft measures that would ensure that those who did not support the appointment of women to the episcopate would not have to come under the authority of a woman bishop. In 2008 the Right Reverend John Broadhurst, Bishop of Fulham, made the telling remark that such measures were necessary for opponents of women bishops to 'live in dignity'. In other words, to be subject to a female in a position of authority within their church's institution was viewed as a loss of dignity, lack of respect, sufficient enough for them to feel that inevitably they were 'being driven out'.[3]

In moving from Christendom to post-Christendom, what might be a helpful way to think of humanity as female and male? As the above examples demonstrate, we come with a legacy of antagonism in terms of the relationship between women and men. We have been bequeathed centuries of perceiving women and men as different and unequal. We live in social structures that are rooted in the practical outworking of such perceptions and the accompanying gender hierarchy and separation, even segregation, of the sexes. The most popular way we have of talking about each other as women and men is in terms of 'the opposite sex', which frequently imagines women and men as adversaries. At other times, our difference, our so-called oppositeness, is presented as complementarity, with a power differential and cultural gender distinctions that determine the proper role, place and function of women and men relative to each other or, more accurately, of women in relation to men.

Daphne Hampson has talked in terms of neighbouring sex[4] – which immediately has the power to change the conversation from language of antagonism to that of good will, and a sense of being side by side rather than in hierarchical relationship. I suggest a similar device, that of women and men as friends, not just or even primarily as individuals, but as a paradigm for thinking about humanity as female and male.

A Hermeneutics of Friendship

I use the term friendship at its contemporary face value with both its negative and positive connotations; friendship is not a state of antagonism, but is a state of mutual regard and indeed affection. While we may talk, of course, of healthy or unhealthy friendships, the analogy of friendship for humanity as female and male is about imagining ourselves as jointly and equally caught up as co-workers in God's human project. Women and men are travellers together, side by side, relating as equals, and not as males above females. As Elaine Storkey says, 'Friends are equals. Real intimacy, in any relationship, depends on an acknowledgment of equality. In fact it can only exist where there is mutuality and reciprocation, and where patterns of dominance and subordination are not exercised.'[5] If we used friendship as an overarching framework (as our hermeneutics) to explore how women and men might relate together in homes, churches and in wider society, might it help us imagine qualitatively different gender relations than those with which we currently wrestle?

The idea of women and men as friends has biblical resonance. 'I have called you friends', Jesus tells his disciples in John's gospel account, and as their friend he talks about how a person's greatest love is to lay their life down for their friends. As Jesus' friends, therefore, united through a common friendship with him, the disciples are also to love one another.[6] Indeed, it may be that 'friend' became a technical term for Christian in the Johannine community.[7]

However, while the notion and practice of friendship was common in the world of the early church, there is no simplistic parallel with our own understanding and habits. That said, attention to some of the differences between ancient and contemporary friendships, in conversation with the New Testament, may help us make use of friendship as a Christian ethic for gender relations today.

Friendship was a broad term in the ancient world covering a range of ideas and practices. While a relationship of mutual virtue and equality was the most perfect form of friendship in Greek thought, this was only possible between aristocratic elites – wealthy, free and of equal status – which inevitably meant only between men. But friendship was also a term that involved differences in power relations, used for bonds between husband and wife, parent and children, and also king and subject, ruler and citizen. As these pairings indicate, for both Greeks and Romans, friendship was also a political tool encompassing relationships of duty, obligation and claims. Establishing a hierarchy of friend-ships to maintain one's power, status and political influence was vital. The Romans even used the language of friendship for the relationship with those from other territories with whom they made treaties or governed as part of their empire.

The Greco-Roman use of friendship clearly overlaps with the patronage system – 'a mutual relationship between unequals for the exchange of services and goods. In addition, the client acquires protection and access to power, while the patron acquires political support where applicable, and prestige and stature in the eyes of others, including peers.'[8] The patronage system, even when couched in the language of friendship, was asymmetrical, the 'softer' language of friendship indicating that the power exchanges between patron and client occurred through personal relationships. Such patronage was a personal relationship, but could have public ramifications. While the vast majority of patrons were men, some wealthy women also acted as public benefactors. It was acceptable for such women to contribute to the good of individuals, social groups or the city from their households as, for example, the New Testament describes Joanna, Lydia and Phoebe as doing.[9]

The friendship Jesus offers to the disciples in the Gospel of John is not of that between equals. It is, however, a personal relation-ship of love that John contrasts with the relationship between slave and master. While the disciples are commanded to follow Jesus, this is encapsulated in the exhortation to love one another, and they do so with an understanding of God's purposes that Christ has made known to them. In John, friendship is 'a principal metaphor for expressing the relationship of redeemed humanity with God'.[10] If women and men are friends of God, they can be friends with one another.

The remarkable thing about this friendship, in all the gospels, is that it is freely offered to all kinds of people that would not have been considered appropriate recipients of friendship or indeed of patronage in the ancient world. The accusation that Jesus was a friend to tax-collectors and sinners was not a compliment but part of the attempts to discredit him.[11] He concerned himself with people who were outcast and marginalized – lepers, beggars, foreigners, those who were poor, ill and disgraced. His friendship made a radical intervention in the social and political mores of his day.

In particular, this practice of friendship works against ancient ideas of male solidarity and this has import for gender relations today. Elizabeth Green argues that, in contrast to patriarchal practices where men collude with each other at women's expense, in the gospels Jesus is shown as publicly undoing such male bonding. She cites several examples, beginning with the exchanges prompted by a woman anointing Jesus.[12]

> In publicly affirming the woman and her action either as a prophetic sign or as a sign of loving recognition, Jesus is shown as deliberately and dramatically disagreeing with Simon's and the disciples' presuppositions. Similarly, the gospel of John depicts Jesus refusing to take sides with the men who were ready to stone the woman taken in adultery as he publicly asks them to consider whether they too might not be guilty. Finally, by refusing to play Pilate or others at their own game of power politics (by coming down from the cross, for example), Jesus is portrayed as rejecting male competition which is the other side of male bonding.[13]

The disruption of this mechanism of patriarchal control is part of the rearranging of relationships required by the new age inaugurated by Jesus, as outlined in Chapter 2. Further, the public nature of these interactions, and indeed the public ramifications of friendship in the ancient world, is an important dimension for our use of a friendship analogy for envisaging contemporary relations between women and men. I propose that envisioning women and men as friends today should not be simply or primarily a matter between private individuals, but a framework for gender relations in all areas of life – both private and public. In other words, I am suggesting friendship as the underlying rationale for how we structure ourselves as women and men in domestic, church and community settings and in wider society. This public dimension also includes offering friendship as part of authentic Christian witness. For in the same way that the gospel is not only of individual relevance but has political and social ramifications, gender relations of friendship may be part of the outworking of our discipleship, a way that we live the good news.

There is one other aspect of Jesus' friendship that is particularly apt for our consideration of women and men after Christendom. The fourth gospel writer who presents us with the picture of Jesus who gathers disciples whom he forms into a group of friends does so against a background of hostility and pressure.

> The Christian community for which St John is writing is evidently a fragile and embattled group, beset on all sides by betrayal, repression and persecution . . . It is a community under pressure, liable to fragmentation; and the evangelist tells the story of Jesus and his disciples in such a way as to encourage the Church of his own time. The miracle of grace, as St John unfolds it, is not so much the miracle of the Good Samaritan, who sacrificially tends the ancestral enemy, but the miracle of friendship within a group of people under pressure to break and run. St Luke tells the story of the 'wideness of God's mercy' that reaches harlot and Pharisee, thief and tax-collector. St John, however, tells the complementary story of the depth of God's mercy that can forge such bonds of love and loyalty within the group that they are prepared even to lay down their lives for one another.[14]

I am not suggesting in any way that our contemporary Western context is parallel to that of John's immediate readers. In Britain, we come from a legacy of Christian influence, control and imposition. We are, however, currently experiencing the shift away from Christendom privilege to living as people of Christian faith in a society of diverse faiths and ideologies that, despite vestiges of favour to Christianity, no longer defers to Christian authority. For a church experiencing the vulnerability of loss of power, there is reason to learn from John's chosen emphasis on friendship as the motif of the corporate identity of believers in a context of uncertainty. And even more than this, the paradigm of friendship is apposite because it offers a qualitatively different approach to a Christendom mindset of power and control from which we are working to break free.

Unmasking Gender Power Relations

Throughout this book I have used the words 'subordinate' and 'subordination' to talk about how women are situated within a (patriarchal and Christendom) hierarchical ordering of gender relations, with men occupying what I have referred to as the 'dominant' position within this arrangement. And I have specifically chosen this wording even when talking about views that frame gender relations in terms of male leadership/responsibility and female following/response, views which are usually talked of in terms of a gender complementarity. Indeed, I have argued that gender complementarity remains a patriarchal construct because it enshrines male authority over women (however benevolently exercised) on the basis of sex: men, because they are men are leaders of women, and women, because they are women are not (and cannot and should not be) leaders of men. It is this organizing – ordering – on the basis of being female and male that is the difficulty with gender hierarchies of whatever name (or of none).

Of course, as human beings we do complement one another – all sorts of us in all sorts of ways. People have diverse and changing abilities, capacities and experiences and can find constructive ways to live and work together in a host of human endeavours. However, when we fix the structure of that complementary working and relating on the basis of sex, we are not simply advocating the principle and practice of human co-operation and harmony. We are, rather, making a particular statement about the nature of women and men and the relationship between them. We are saying that the sex of a person, rather than the character and gifting of individual women and men, initially determines their eligibility to do certain jobs, carry out certain roles, hold particular offices, or lead families and households. And we are saying that, however worked out, men by virtue of their maleness have authority over women and not the other way around.

Having said that, some who espouse a gender complementarity do incorporate women's gifting in many ways in, for example, church settings, including leadership and teaching of both women and men if the women concerned are ultimately under male authority. We might ask, therefore, whether what view of gender we hold makes much difference in practice. Is this more a theoretical question than a real one? It does matter, however, because we are not just talking about what women may or may not do, but about how they see themselves – and are seen by men. It concerns the way women behave, how they exercise their gifts, and how they relate to others. In other words, this is not just about what women can and cannot do, but the accompanying gender expectations involving a value system and cultural construct about the nature of being female and male. These constructions of femininity and masculinity are rooted in a notion of female and male as not simply different in certain ways but as opposite, even though that opposition may be renamed as complementarity. This becomes evident when people support the notion of merit and gifting of women while also holding onto a divinely ordained male leadership. While decrying any implication of women's inferiority, instead the divine order is explained by appealing to women's natural (created) disposition to certain roles and ways of being and relating.

Our view of gender relations matters, too, because it impacts on men as well as women. Any form of gender hierarchy leaves intact a construction of male identity that requires women to be subordinate on the basis of their femaleness, claiming this has divine sanction. Hence, moving from a view of gender complementarity, which will mean removing the mindsets and structures that subordinate women, involves change for men as much as it does for women. Even men who do not share a mindset (the way we think and view the world) of patriarchal gender order nevertheless experience living in its structures (how such thinking is embedded in our social organization). Living free of the constraints of gender order is rare for women or men.

Further, views on gender relations matter because they play a crucial role in our Christian imagination. God is characterized through near-exclusive male imagery including, and perhaps even in particular, the metaphor of male personal pronouns (God as 'he'). This practice of treating God as male, even while (usually) in theory holding God is neither female nor male, is bound up in notions of a God–man–woman hierarchy. Dominant Christian imagination suggests that maleness is more akin to divinity than femaleness. The objection to using female imagery to refer to God further reinforces this, many finding the idea of God as 'she' emotive and disturbing, indicating how deep-seated is gendered imaging of the divine.

This gendered Christian imagination in turn impacts on our self-understandings and gendered social relations. The gospel is then worked out differently in the lives of women *in relation to* men. Women Christians' discipleship comes to endorse male priority and privilege, foster women's service and even condone their suffering. In other words, particular constructions of femininity and masculinity come to define what following Jesus means for women and men, and women in relation to men, rather than Christian discipleship shaping not only what kind of women and men we are but the relational dynamic between women and men.

Support for androcentric Christian imagination (that is, male-centred imagining of God) and its accompanying gender hierarchy is said to come from the Bible's own use of male terms for God. Here we are confronted with a question of hermeneutics – how do we interpret the text? How do we come from our world to its world and make meaning out of this encounter? Part of reading the Bible with a post-Christendom awareness is to be alert for how mainstream and marginal, powerful and powerless voices are present in the text and in interpretations of it. Is it not centuries of patriarchal dominance that mean more is read into the Bible's male imagery than the fact that it was predominantly produced out of patriarchal contexts? To infer sanction of a gender hierarchy from the male language used goes against the text's own witness. For the text itself (even *in* its androcentric language) contains evidence that male metaphors for God are not to be understood as conferring particular patriarchal constructs onto God. So, Jesus' use of God as father undermines all kinds of earthly hierarchies and speaks against systems of domination. As does the idea of the kingdom of God whose king is unlike earthly rulers. The task remains of working out how to use both of these terms (God as father and the kingdom of God) in our Christian communities today in a way that retains rather than subverts their original significance.

Thinking about how gender power relations function to structure our thoughts and lives matters because without giving this some attention we lack the ability to change things. This may be true even for those keen to enact different gender practices that do not define and confine on the basis of a patriarchal gender hierarchy. For only changing rules or giving formal permissions for different practice may be relatively ineffective if the underlying cultures and socialization are not also given attention. This culture and socialization includes private and public as well as ecclesial domains and it involves personal relationships and personal identities. Our sense of ourselves is enmeshed in gender power relations and there may be as much invested for some people (both women and men) in keeping the status quo as in changing it. While Scripture and tradition may be the presenting arguments for maintaining a gender hierarchy, none of us is a neutral commentator on these sources. A key question for each person to ask is, 'What is at stake for me here?' Often issues of personal worth and place are caught up in our stance on gender relations; this is as true for women as it is for men, but that does not mean all women are alike in their responses any more than all men will be.

The complicated and deep-rooted entanglement of our own identities in our stance on gender relations means that even apparent superficial or simple changes in practice may be disquieting. So for example, while, in many worship and church community contexts, we *may* be able to start using, without any particular explanation, gender-inclusive language as our default for speaking of humanity, the same may not be so for our imaging of God.[15] Apart from the misdirection of occasional gender-inclusive God-talk (in that *occasional* use of gender-inclusive or female metaphors tends to reinforce that talking about God in male metaphors is the norm), there is also insufficient consciousness of the nature of all metaphorical language for God, let alone the way our language for God has been used to both reflect and reinforce gender relations.[16] It should not be surprising, therefore, if there are visceral responses even to the *idea* of reflecting on the impact of our God-talk on women and men. How we explore our God-talk is a pastoral as well as prophetic[17] and theological matter.

Even using gender-inclusive terms for humanity can meet with irritation or resistance. In this regard 'political correctness' applied to attempts to speak inclusively is more often used derogatively than it is descriptively. It is commonplace to deride attempts to change familiar gender-exclusive ways of speaking of people. However, while there may be occasions where political correctness is applied legalistically and loses the spirit of its intent, this is no reason to abandon the project of speaking well and carefully about one another. 'Seeing speech as a kind of action'[18] reminds us that rendering women linguistically invisible does impact on the way women and men experience the world, and the way they relate to one another.

The suggestion that we are wise to tread carefully in disman-tling hierarchical gender practices is not the same thing as saying we take no steps at all. To do nothing is to continue to perpetuate injustice in our gender relations. However, because much of that injustice is 'normal' habit and practice, it often goes unnoticed. Indeed, it is so much ingrained in our notions of stability and what is right, that challenges to it become characterized as intro-ducing potential discrimination or injury.

To give a prominent example, there has been much discussion over recent decades about the possibility that people (both women and men, and particularly male priests and bishops) might leave the Church of England with the admission of women to ordained offices (of deacon, priest and bishop). Concern for those individual ministers and parishes that might leave, and for the harm to the unity of the whole church if they were to do so, has been a major theme, along with concerns about relationships with other church institutions who do not support women's ordination. What this particular argument omits, however, is that people are already leaving and harm is already being done because of women's exclusion and what the supporting rationale says about women.

Similarly, as with the example at the start of this chapter, in some Catholic parishes, the analysis that boys may not come forward to be altar servers if girls are admitted leaves unexamined what is being said about girls in either their exclusion or admission. Embedded injustice, of whatever kind, disguises itself as norma-tive and challenge to this injustice may itself become character-ized as damaging.

Without giving attention to gender power relations, we risk replicating them even in initiatives that appear to be innovative. The outworking of the concern (rather than the concern itself), through contemporary versions of muscular Christianity, to engage men in churches is one such example. Men's movements that emphasize so-called masculine characteristics of God and of men perpetuate notions of male separation and difference from femaleness. This is not to make an argument against female- or male-only groups or gatherings; these may be beneficial and even necessary from time to time or as part of ongoing practice. It is, rather, to ask about the wider purpose that such groups serve. Nor does this overall argument mean there is no such thing as femininity or masculinity. It is, however, to maintain these are changeable cultural constructions rather than permanent givens and should not perpetuate gender injustice. And it is not to say that sexual distinction and physical embodiment are irrelevant or that these, along with our gendered social embodiment, make no particular contributions to personal, community or public relationships. But it is to question whether a difference of structured gender opposites, including that of subordination and dominance, should be allowed to shape the social relations of women and men. It is to argue that our sense of ourselves does not have to be constructed at the expense of another person.

Women, Men and the Gospel

A commonly expressed idea is that matters concerning gender – which often are phrased as issues about women's role or women in leadership – are not core theological concerns. What this, in effect, means is that gender relations becomes something on which Christians may disagree without it, in theory, jeopardizing their sense of community and belonging. It is sometimes different when the disagreement is focused around biblical interpretation and the pivotal question then presents itself as being about biblical *authority*, which for some is viewed as core to Christian orthodoxy. It is also the case, as a hermeneutics of suspicion reminds us, that it is easier for those in dominant positions or personally fulfilling situations (whether female or male) to claim that our stance on gender is a secondary concern than it is, for example, for women who find themselves invisible in liturgies, blocked from applying for certain jobs, confined by gendered expectations, judged more harshly than their male colleagues, laughed at for raising their concerns, or viewed as sexually dangerous.[19]

Another frequently expressed idea is that matters concerning gender are considered relatively unimportant in the long list of things that require attention in churches and not especially relevant to gospel proclamation. In effect, this means they are ignored, which largely means the continuation of an unexamined patriarchal status quo. Even the possibility of considering gender relations is thus circumscribed; and this containment is further supported by underscoring appropriate Christian demeanours of humility and service and the so-called bigger picture of the priority of the gospel.

Clearly, from my argument in this book, I do not agree that gender relations are not core theological or gospel concerns. The status of a woman's or a man's personhood before God seems to me fundamentally and irreducibly to be part of the gospel. To view matters of gender as about, for example, women's rights and therefore to be about unacceptable Christian behaviour of self-assertion, is to misconstrue what is at stake. It is also not to see how gender relations are currently caught up in the gospel in that, for example, our dominant gender order is often endorsed by Christian calls for self-sacrifice and self-denial. Our outworking of the gospel already is enmeshed in our practice of gender relations and, hence, to subject the latter to scrutiny is not to introduce a new concern into Christian praxis but to examine an existing one.

Of course, it is sometimes said that a person's standing before God is not what is involved in the different views on gender relations. Put another way, that a woman's or a man's spiritual standing depends on their relationship to God and not their relationship to one another. This is not to ignore necessarily the importance of 'working out our salvation'[20] – for right relationship with God leads to our seeking to restore right relationships with each other – but it does tend to present a linear progression from spiritual to social reconciliation and to prioritize the former. However, if our behaviour towards others (on a personal or societal level) is the embodiment of our right relationship with God, then these are not two distinct sets of relationships but rather form an integrated whole. 'Salvation understood in terms of reconciliation has to do with overcoming alienation between God and ourselves in a way that is inseparable from restoring human relationships and therefore human well-being.'[21] While we may be able to identify various elements involved, sense and meaning is found when we hold onto and understand the integrated whole.

What will these new, restored or non-hierarchical gender relationships look like? Given the variety of human cultures and situations, there will be different forms and patterns of what it means for women and men to be friends of Jesus and of each other – to use one of the hermeneutics available to us. This diversity in itself can be unsettling or feel threatening. The uncertainties and anxieties attached to anything unknown or untried can lead to a preference for remaining within the familiar. This is no less so with our re-imagining of gender relations. Without specific models to follow, some people may be unwilling to enter into new relational dynamics and practices. However, gender relations after Christendom is an imaginative venture that requires innovation, diversity and challenge.

It is the task of Christian communities to explore what this means: to seek to understand the dynamics of our gendered lives so that we move beyond superficial responses; to find appropriate ways to lament harmful gender attitudes and practices as part of a process of both healing and reorienting to a new way of relating; and to do what is required to bring into being the hope of the gospel for restored relationships between women and men.

Bibliography

Annesley, Claire, and Francesca Gains. 'The Core Executive: Gender, Power and Change'. *Political Studies* 58 (2010): pp. 909–29.

Archbishops' Council. 'Statistics for Mission 2012: Ministry'. Archbishops' Council, Research and Statistics, Central Secretariat: London (2013) http://www.churchofengland.org/media/1868964/ministry%20statistics%20final.pdf (accessed 18 Nov. 2013).

Armstrong, Karen. *The Gospel According to Women* (London: Fount, 1986).

Arnold, Patrick. *Wildmen, Warriors and Kings* (New York: Crossroad, 1991).

Aston, Margaret. 'Segregation in Church.' Pages 237–94 in *Studies in Church History Volume 27: Women in the Church* (ed. W.J. Sheils and Diana Wood; Oxford: Basil Blackwell, 1990).

Atkinson, Peter. *Friendship and the Body of Christ* (London: SPCK, 2004).

Bailey, Kenneth E. 'Women in the New Testament: A Middle Eastern Cultural View'. *Theology Matters* 6 (2000): pp. 1–11.

— *Paul Through Mediterranean Eyes: Cultural Studies in 1 Corinthians* (London: SPCK, 2011).

Bainton, Roland H. *Christian Attitudes to War and Peace* (London: Hodder & Stoughton, 1961).

Barrett, C.K. *The Gospel According to John* (London: SPCK, 2nd edn, 1978).

Bauman-Martin, Betsy J. 'Women on the Edge: New Perspectives on Women in the Petrine Haustafel', *Journal of Biblical Literature* 123/2 (1995).

Beal, Becky. 'The Promise Keepers' Use of Sport in Defining "Christlike" Masculinity'. *Journal of Sport and Social Issues* 21 (1997): pp. 274–84.

Belleville, Linda L. '1 Timothy.' Pages 734–47 in *The IVP Women's Bible Commentary* (ed. Catherine Clark Kroeger and Mary Evans; Downers Grove, IL: InterVarsity Press, 2002).

Bettenson, Henry. *Documents of the Christian Church* (Oxford: Oxford University Press, 2nd edn, 1963).

Bly, Robert. *Iron John: A Book About Men* (Reading, MA: Addison-Wesley, 1990).

Boyd, Stephen B., W. Merle Longwood and Mark W. Muesse. 'Men, Masculinity and the Study of Religion.' Pages xiii-xxii in *Redeeming Men, Religions and Masculinities* (ed. Stephen B. Boyd, W. Merle Longwood and Mark W. Muesse; Louisville, KY: Westminster John Knox Press, 1996).

Brock, Rita Nakashima, and Rebecca Ann Parker. *Saving Paradise: How Christianity Traded Love of This World for Crucifixion and Empire* (Boston: Beacon Press, 2008).

Brown, Peter Robert Lamont. *The Body and Society: Men, Women, and Sexual Renunciation in Early Christianity* (New York: Columbia University Press, 1988).

Bruce, F.F. *The Epistle of Paul to the Galatians: A Commentary on the Greek Text* (Exeter: Paternoster Press, 1982).

Clack, Beverley. 'The Denial of Dualism: Thealogical Reflections on the Sexual and the Spiritual'. *Feminist Theology* (1995): pp. 102–15.

Clague, Julie. 'The Christa: Symbolizing My Humanity and My Pain'. *Feminist Theology* 14.1 (2005): pp. 83–108.

— 'Interview with Margaret Argyle'. *Feminist Theology* 10 (1995): pp. 57–68.

Clanton, Jann Aldredge. *In Whose Image? God and Gender* (London: SCM, 1990).

Cohick, Lynn H. *Women in the World of the Earliest Christians: Illuminating Ancient Ways of Life* (Grand Rapids, MI: Baker Academic, 2009).

Cole, Edwin Louis. *Maximized Manhood* (New Kensington, PA: Whitaker House, 1982).

Daly, Mary. *Beyond God the Father* (London: Women's Press, 1986).

De Gruchy, John W. *Being Human: Confessions of a Christian Humanist* (London: SCM Press, 2006).

Donegan-Cross, Guy. *Men and God* (Cambridge: Grove Books, 2000).

Dungan, David L. *Constantine's Bible: Politics and the Making of the New Testament* (London: SCM Press, 2006).

Eisen, Ute E. *Women Officeholders in Early Christianity: Epigraphical and Literary Studies* (Collegeville, MN: Liturgical Press, 2000).

Eldredge, John. *Wild at Heart: Discovering the Secret of a Man's Soul* (Nashville, TN: Thomas Nelson, 2001).

Equal Opportunities Commission. 'Greater Expecations. Summary Final Report, EOC's Investigation into Pregnancy Discrimination'. (2005).

Equality and Human Rights Commission. 'Working Better: Fathers, Family and Work – Contemporary Perspectives'. *Research Summary* 41 (Manchester: Equality and Human Rights Commission, 2009).

Eusebius, *Proof of the Gospel* 1:48–9, http://www.ccel.org/ccel/pearse/morefathers/files/eusebius_de_03_book1.htm (accessed 8 May 2010).

Fiorenza, Elisabeth Schüssler. *In Memory of Her: A Feminist Theological Reconstruction of Christian Origins* (London: SCM, 1983).

— *The Power of the Word: Scripture and the Rhetoric of Empire* (Minneapolis: Fortress Press, 2007).

Fleming, Jacky. *Be a Bloody Train Driver* (London: Penguin, 1991).

France, R.T. *Women in the Church's Ministry: A Test-Case for Biblical Hermeneutics* (Carlisle, UK: Paternoster Press, 1995).

Gelfer, Joseph. 'Evangelical and Catholic Masculinities in Two Fatherhood Ministries'. *Feminist Theology* 19 (2010): pp. 36–53.

— 'Identifying the Catholic Men's Movement'. *Journal of Men's Studies* 16 (2008): pp. 41–56.

Gibbon, Margaret. *Feminist Perspectives on Language* (London and New York: Longman, 1999).

Good, Deirdre. *Jesus' Family Values* (New York: Church Publishing, 2006).

Graham, Elaine. 'Gender.' Pages 78–80 in *An A to Z of Feminist Theology* (ed. Lisa Isherwood and Dorothea McEwan; Sheffield: Sheffield Academic Press, 1996).

— *Making the Difference: Gender, Personhood and Theology* (London: Mowbray, 1995).

Green, Elizabeth. 'More Musings on Maleness: The Maleness of Jesus Revisited'. *Feminist Theology* 20 (1999): pp. 9–27.

Gritz, Sharon Hodgin. *Paul, Women Teachers, and the Mother Goddess at Ephesus: A Study of I Timothy 2:9–15 in the Light of the Religious and Cultural Milieu of the First Century* (Lanham, MD: University Press of America, 1991).

Groothuis, Rebecca Merrill, and Douglas Groothuis. 'Women Keep Promises, Too!'. *Priscilla Papers* 11 (1997): pp. 1–9.

Hagan, Kay Leigh. 'Introduction.' Pages xi-xiv in *Women Respond to the Men's Movement* (ed. Kay Leigh Hagan; San Francisco: Pandora, 1992).

Hampson, Daphne. *After Christianity* (London: SCM Press Ltd, 1996).

Hart, David Bentley. *Atheist Delusions* (New Haven and London: Yale University Press, 2009).

Hauerwas, Stanley. *After Christendom* (Nashville, TN: Abingdon Press, 1991).

Heath, Melanie. 'Soft-Boiled Masculinity: Renegotiating Gender and Racial Ideologies in the Promise Keepers Movement'. *Gender & Society* 17 (2003): pp. 423–44.

Hilkert, Mary Catherine. 'Key Religious Symbols: Christ and God'. *Theological Studies* 56 (1995): pp. 341–52.

Hogan, Linda. *Human Rights* (Dublin and London: Trocaire; Veritas; and CAFOD, 1998).

Holdsworth, Angela. *Out of the Doll's House* (London: BBC Books, 1988).

Hughes, Thomas. *The Manliness of Christ* (London: Macmillan, 1879).

Isherwood, Lisa. 'Editorial'. *Feminist Theology* 19 (1998): pp. 5–9.

Jensen, Anne. *God's Self-Confident Daughters: Early Christianity and the Liberation of Women* (Kampen, The Netherlands: Kok Pharos, 1996).

Johnson, Elizabeth A. *She Who Is: The Mystery of God in Feminist Theological Discourse* (New York: Crossroad, 1997).

Judge, Edwin Arthur. *The Social Pattern of the Christian Groups in the First Century* (Tyndale Press: London, 1960).

Kraemer, Ross Shepard. *Her Share of the Blessings: Women's Religions among Pagans, Jews, and Christians in the Greco-Roman World* (New York; Oxford: Oxford University Press, 1992).

Kreider, Alan. *The Change of Conversion and the Origin of Christendom* (Eugene, Origen: Wipf & Stock, 1999).

Kroeger, Catherine Clark, Mary Evans, and Elaine Storkey, eds.
Women's Study New Testament (London: Marshall Pickering,
1995).

Kroeger, Catherine Clark, and Nancy Nason-Clark, *No Place for
Abuse: Biblical and Practical Resources to Counteract Domestic
Violence* (Downers Grove, IL: InterVarsity Press, 2001).

Kroeger, Richard Clark, and Catherine Clark Kroeger. *I Suffer Not a
Woman: Rethinking 1 Timothy 2:11–15 in Light of Ancient Evidence*
(Grand Rapids, MI: Baker, 1992).

Lane, Tony. *The Lion Concise Book of Christian Thought* (Tring, Herts:
Lion, 1984).

Leyser, Conrad. 'Custom, Truth, and Gender in Eleventh-Century
Reform.' Pages 75–91 in *Gender and Christian Religion* (ed. R.N.
Swanson; Woodbridge, Suffolk: Boydell & Brewer, 1998).

MacCulloch, Diarmaid. *A History of Christianity: The First Three
Thousand Years* (London: Allen Lane, 2009).

— *Reformation: Europe's House Divided 1490–1700* (London:
Penguin, 2004).

MacDonald, Margaret Y. *Early Christian Women and Pagan Opinion:
The Power of the Hysterical Woman* (Cambridge: Cambridge
University Press, 1996).

— 'Was Celsus Right? The Role of Women in the Expansion of
Early Christianity.' Pages 157–84 in *Early Christian Families in
Context: An Interdisciplinary Dialogue* (ed. David L Balch and
Carolyn Osiek; Grand Rapids, MI: Eerdmans, 2003).

Macy, Gary. *The Hidden History of Women's Ordination: Female Clergy
in the Medieval West* (New York: Oxford University Press, 2008).

Miller-McLemore, Bonnie J. *Also a Mother: Work and Family as Theological Dilemma* (Nashville, TN: Abingdon Press, 1994).

Morley, Patrick. 'The Next Christian Men's Movement'. *Christianity Today*, 4 September 2000.

Murray, Stuart. *The Naked Anabaptist* (Scottdale, PA/Waterloo,
Ontario: Herald Press, 2010).

— *Post-Christendom* (Carlisle: Paternoster, 2004).

— 'Post-Christendom, Post-Constantinian, Post-Christian . . .
Does the Label Matter?' http://www.anabaptistnetwork.com/
book/export/html/506 (accessed 1 Feb. 2010).

Murray Williams, Stuart and Sian. *Multi-Voiced Church* (Milton Keynes: Paternoster, 2012).

Osiek, Carolyn, and David L. Balch, *Families in the New Testament World: Households and House Churches* (Louisville, KY: Westminster John Knox Press, 1997).

Paul, Ian. 'Women, Teaching and Authority.' Pages 33–44 in *Women and Men in Scripture and the Church: A Guide to Key Issues* (ed. Steven Croft and Paula Gooder; Norwich: Canterbury Press, 2013).

Phillips, Anne. *The Faith of Girls: Children's Spirituality and Transition to Adulthood* (Farnham: Ashgate, 2011).

Pietersen, Lloyd. *Reading the Bible after Christendom* (Milton Keynes: Paternoster, 2011).

Porter, Fran. *Changing Women, Changing Worlds: Evangelical Women in Church, Community and Politics* (Belfast: Blackstaff, 2002).

— *It Will Not Be Taken Away from Her: A Feminist Engagement with Women's Christian Experience* (London: Darton, Longman & Todd, 2004).

Procter-Smith, Marjorie. ' "Reorganizing Victimization": The Intersection between Liturgy and Domestic Violence.' Pages 380–95 in *Christian Perspectives on Sexuality and Gender* (ed. Adrian Thatcher and Elizabeth Stuart; Leominster: Gracewing, 1996).

Pugh, S.S. *Christian Manliness: A Book of Examples and Principles for Young Men* (London: Religious Tract Society, 1867).

Rake, Katherine, and Rowena Lewis. 'Just Below the Surface: Gender Stereotyping, the Silent Barrier to Equality in the Modern Workplace?' (London: Fawcett Society, 2009) http://www.fawcettsociety.org.uk/documents/Just%20Below%20the%20Surface.pdf (accessed 12 Oct. 2009).

Ramshaw, Gail. 'The Gender of God.' Pages 168–80 in *Feminist Theology: A Reader* (ed. Ann Loades; London: SPCK, 1990).

Randall, Margaret. ' "And So She Walked Over and Kissed Him . . ." Robert Bly's Men's Movement.' Pages 141–8 in *Women Respond to the Men's Movement* (ed. Kay Leigh Hagan; San Francisco: Pandora, 1992).

Ranke-Heinemann, Uta. *Eunuchs for the Kingdom of Heaven: The Catholic Church and Sexuality* (London: Penguin, 1990).

Riggs, Marcia Y. 'Equality.' Pages 84–5 in *Dictionary of Feminist Theologies* (ed. Letty M. Russell and J. Shannon Clarkson; London: Mowbray, 1996).

Roper, Lyndal. ' "The Common Man", "the Common Good", "Common Women": Gender and Meaning in the German Reformation Commune'. *Social History* 12 (1987): pp. 1–21.

— 'Sexual Utopianism in the German Reformation'. *Journal of Ecclesiastical History*, 42 (1991): pp. 394–418.

Ruether, Rosemary Radford. *Christianity and the Making of the Modern Family* (London: SCM Press, 2001).

— 'Patriarchy and the Men's Movement: Part of the Problem or Part of the Solution?' Pages 13–18 in *Women Respond to the Men's Movement* (ed. Kay Leigh Hagan; San Francisco: Pandora, 1992).

— 'Patriarchy.' Pages 173–4 in *An A to Z of Feminist Theology* (ed. Lisa Isherwood and Dorothea McEwan; Sheffield: Sheffield Academic Press, 1996).

Schmidt, Alvin John. *Veiled and Silenced: How Culture Shaped Sexist Theology* (Macon, GA: Mercer University Press, 1989).

Scholer, David M. '1 Timothy 2:9–15 & the Place of Women in the Church's Ministry.' Pages 193–219 in *Women, Authority and the Bible* (ed. Alvera Mickelsen; Basingstoke: Marshall Pickering, 1987).

Shaw, Jane. 'Gender and the Act of Synod.' Pages 14–26 in *Act of Synod – Act of Folly?* (ed. Monica Furlong; London: SCM, 1998).

Slee, Nicola. *Seeking the Risen Christa* (London: SPCK, 2011).

Snyder, C. Arnold, and Linda A. Huebert Hecht, eds. *Profiles of Anabaptist Women: Sixteenth Century Reforming Pioneers* (Waterloo, ON, Canada: Wilfrid Laurier University Press, 1996).

Spencer, Aída Besançon. *1 Timothy: A New Covenant Commentary* (Eugene, OR: Cascade Books, 2013).

Spender, Dale. *Man Made Language* (London: Pandora, 2nd edn, 1994).

Starhawk. 'A Men's Movement I Can Trust.' Pages 27–37 in *Women Respond to the Men's Movement* (ed. Kay Leigh Hagan; San Francisco: Pandora, 1992).

Stark, Rodney. *The Rise of Christianity: How the Obscure, Marginal Jesus Movement Became the Dominant Religious Force in the Western World in a Few Centuries* (San Francisco: Harper Collins, 1997).

Stein, Arlene. 'Make Room for Daddy: Anxious Masculinity and Emergent Homophobias in Neopatriarchal Politics'. *Gender & Society* 19 (2005): pp. 601–20.

Stjerna, Kirsi. *Women and the Reformation* (New York: Wiley-Blackwell, 2009).

Storkey, Elaine. *The Search for Intimacy* (London: Hodder & Stoughton, 1995).

Stratton, Beverly J. 'Eve through Several Lenses: Truth in 1 Timothy 2.8–15.' Pages 258–73 in *A Feminist Companion to the Hebrew Bible in the New Testament* (ed. Athalya Brenner; Sheffield: Sheffield Academic Press, 1996).

Swartley, Willard M. Slavery, *Sabbath, War and Women: Case Issues in Biblical Interpretation* (Scottdale, PA: Herald Press, 1983).

Tamez, Elsa. *Struggles for Power in Early Christianity: A Study of the First Letter to Timothy* (trans. Gloria Kinsler; Maryknoll, NY: Orbis Books, 2007 [2005]).

Thiselton, Anthony C. 'Hermeneutics.' Pages 293–7 in *New Dictionary of Theology* (ed. Sinclair B. Ferguson and David F. Wright; Leicester, England: Inter-Varsity Press, 1988).

Thompson, Marianne Meye. *The Promise of the Father: Jesus and God in the New Testament* (Louisville, KY: Westminster John Knox Press, 2000).

Trevett, Christine. 'Gender, Authority and Church History: A Case Study of Montanism'. *Feminst Theology* (1998): pp. 9–24.

Tucker, Ruth A., and Walter L. Liefeld. *Daughters of the Church: Women and Ministry from New Testament Times to the Present* (Grand Rapids, MI: Academie Books, 1987).

Van Leeuwen, Mary Stewart, ed. *After Eden: Facing the Challenge of Gender Reconciliation* (Grand Rapids, MI: Eerdmans, 1993).

— *Gender and Grace: Women and Men in a Changing World* (Inter-Varsity Press: Leicester, 1990).

— 'Servanthood or Soft Patriarchy?'. *Priscilla Papers* 11 (1997): pp. 28–40.

Wiesner, Merry E. *Women and Gender in Early Modern Europe* (Cambridge: Cambridge University Press, 2nd edn, 2000).

Wijngaards, John. *Women Deacons in the Early Church: Historical Texts and Contemporary Debates* (New York: Crossroad Publishing Company, 2006).

Woodhead, Linda. 'Sex and Secularization.' Pages 230–44 in *Queer Theology: Rethinking the Western Body* (ed. Gerard Loughlin; Oxford: Blackwell, 2007).

Woodroffe, Jessica. 'Not Having It All: How Motherhood Reduces Women's Pay and Employment Prospects' (London: Fawcett Society, 2009) http://www.fawcettsociety.org.uk/documents/NotHavingItAll.pdf (accessed 3 Dec. 2010).

Wren, Brian. *What Language Shall I Borrow? God Talk in Worship: A Male Response to Feminist Theology* (London: SCM, 1989).

Yoder, John Howard. *The Politics of Jesus* (Grand Rapids, MI: Eerdmans, 1972).

Endnotes

Introduction

[1] Lyndal Roper, 'Sexual Utopianism in the German Reformation', *Journal of Ecclesiastical History* 42 (1991): p. 395.

[2] Robert Bly, *Iron John: A Book About Men* (Reading, MA: Addison-Wesley, 1990).

1. Thinking Beyond Christendom's Gender

[1] Succession to the Crown Bill, 2013.

[2] Stuart Murray, 'Series Preface.' Page vii of this book.

[3] Stuart Murray, *The Naked Anabaptist* (Scottdale, PA/Waterloo, Ontario: Herald Press, 2010), p. 73.

[4] Stuart Murray, *Post-Christendom* (Carlisle: Paternoster, 2004), p. 19.

[5] Murray, *Post-Christendom*, p. 20.

[6] Stanley Hauerwas, *After Christendom* (Nashville, TN: Abingdon Press, 1991), p. 18. Stanley Hauerwas is using Constantinianism for the same phenomenon as Christendom, although a debate exists as to the appropriateness of the term. See Stuart Murray, 'Post-Christendom, Post-Constantinian, Post-Christian . . . Does the Label Matter?' http://www.anabaptistnetwork.com/book/export/html/506 (accessed 1 Feb. 2010).

[7] David L. Dungan, *Constantine's Bible: Politics and the Making of the New Testament* (London: SCM Press, 2006), pp. 19, 14.

[8] Diarmaid MacCulloch, *A History of Christianity: The First Three Thousand Years* (London: Allen Lane, 2009), p. 26.

[9] Dungan, *Constantine' Bible*.

[10] Or, similarly, 'Hardy and Laurel', 'Sullivan and Gilbert'.

[11] Rosemary Radford Ruether, 'Patriarchy', in *An A to Z of Feminist Theology* (ed. Lisa Isherwood and Dorothea McEwan; Sheffield: Sheffield Academic Press, 1996), p. 174.

[12] Elisabeth Schüssler Fiorenza, *The Power of the Word: Scripture and the Rhetoric of Empire* (Minneapolis: Fortress Press, 2007), p. 14.

[13] Emotional housework – also called emotional labour, particularly when performed in contexts outside the home and family – is a way of referring to the fact that women take care of a family's emotional life and needs (attending to how people feel; maintaining relationships; and remembering birthdays and anniversaries, which can include reminding a husband it is his mother's birthday coming up, buying presents on behalf of household members to give to others, and sending the Christmas cards) in the same way that traditionally they have taken care of practicalities in the house (cooking, cleaning, ironing, shopping and organizing).

[14] Mary Stewart Van Leeuwen, *Gender and Grace: Women and Men in a Changing World* (IVP: Leicester, 1990), pp. 113–4. This example is taken from her own fieldwork in West Africa.

[15] Mary Stewart Van Leeuwen, ed., *After Eden: Facing the Challenge of Gender Reconciliation* (Eerdmans: Grand Rapids, MI, 1993), p. 22.

[16] Transgender is a term that reflects the changing uses of the words sex and gender and generally is a more encompassing term for transgender experience and identity than transsexual. See also footnote 19.

[17] Elaine Graham, *Making the Difference. Gender, Personhood and Theology* (London: Mowbray, 1995), p. 144.

[18] Elaine Graham, 'Gender', in *An A to Z of Feminist Theology* (ed. Lisa Isherwood and Dorothea McEwan; Sheffield: Sheffield Academic Press, 1996), p. 80.

[19] LGBT is a common term among support, advocacy and campaigning groups for lesbian, gay, bisexual and/or transgender people. Gay is preferred to the term homosexual given the often narrow use of the latter to refer to sexual activity and to its association with pathology (an illness needing clinical correction). Gay and lesbian are more holistic terms that speak of people in the entirety of their identity, which includes same-sex attraction but in a way that does not sexualize or sexually objectify people. Similarly the term transgender is preferred to transsexual (both of which are used as adjectives and not nouns) because it focuses on gender identity rather than on sexual identity.

20 Anthony C. Thiselton, 'Hermeneutics', in *New Dictionary of Theology* (ed. Sinclair B. Ferguson and David F. Wright; Leicester, England: Inter-Varsity Press, 1988), p. 293.

21 The term 'hermeneutics' may be used as both plural and singular (rather than 'hermeneutic'). I use the plural form as a reminder that each particular form of hermeneutics (such as justice or suspicion) can itself contain diversity and be applied differently in a variety of contexts (for example, what particular injustice is being addressed; what particular power relations need to be examined).

22 Murray, *Post-Christendom*, p. 248.

23 We may work with a number of hermeneutics at the same time, for example, employing a hermeneutics of suspicion (Chapter 6), a hermeneutics of justice, and a hermeneutics of friendship, allowing each to speak to the others.

24 Luke 10:25–37.

2. Women and Men Before Christendom

1 Tony Lane, *The Lion Concise Book of Christian Thought* (Tring, Herts: Lion, 1984), p. 10.

2 Lane, *Lion Concise Book*, p. 10.

3 Epistle to the Corinthians xliii and xlii–xliv, cited in Henry Bettenson, *Documents of the Christian Church* (Oxford: OUP, 2nd edn, 1963), pp. 32–3. Initially the understanding of apostolic succession was about the authority of Christian teaching and tradition because of the demonstrable links with the apostles, rather than a sacramental understanding which developed later.

4 Epistle to the Smyrnaeans 8, cited in Bettenson, *Documents*, pp. 63f.

5 As Chapter 3 outlines, the understanding and practice of this three-fold pattern changed and developed through the centuries. Hence, while there is continuity between contemporary meanings and ancient patterns, there are also differences.

6 Rosemary Radford Ruether, *Christianity and the Making of the Modern Family* (London: SCM Press, 2001), p. 13.

7 Exemptions from male guardianship for emancipated women were introduced by Augustus (through *lex Julia* around 18 BC and *lex Papia Poppaea* in AD 9) if a woman had three (for a free-born Roman citizen) or four (for a freedwoman) live births, defined as a child surviving to

the naming ceremony (eight days after birth for a girl and nine days for a boy). Lynn H Cohick, *Women in the World of the Earliest Christians: Illuminating Ancient Ways of Life* (Grand Rapids, MI: Baker, 2009), pp. 42–3, 108, 124–5.

[8] One of the privileges of being in the female Roman priesthood of Vestal Virgins (an exclusive group believed to compromise of no more than six women at any one time) was freedom from any male guardianship. Ross Shepard Kraemer, *Her Share of the Blessings: Women's Religions Among Pagans, Jews, and Christians in the Greco-Roman World* (New York, Oxford: OUP, 1992), p. 81.

[9] Ruether, *Christianity and the Making of the Modern Family*, p. 14.

[10] Deirdre Good, *Jesus' Family Values* (New York: Church Publishing, 2006), p. 36.

[11] F.F. Bruce, *The Epistle of Paul to the Galatians: A Commentary on the Greek Text* (Exeter: Paternoster Press, 1982), p. 197.

[12] Rom. 8:12–17; Gal. 4:4–7.

[13] Cohick, *Women in the World of the Earliest Christians*, pp. 81–2, 131.

[14] It is not known if Jewish practice followed the biblical injunction to free a Jewish slave after six years and, if so, if this applied to women. Cohick, *Women in the World of the Earliest Christians*, p. 279.

[15] Cohick, *Women in the World of the Earliest Christians*, p. 22.

[16] Ruether, *Christianity and the Making of the Modern Family*, p. 19.

[17] Matt. 18:23–35 (parable of the unforgiving servant); Matt. 20:1–16 (parable of the landowner and hired labourers); Matt. 21:33–41 (parable of the landowner and tenants); Matt. 24:45–51 and Luke 12:41–8 (parable of the faithful and unfaithful slaves); Matt. 25:14–30 (parable of the talents); Luke 14:15–24 (parable of the great dinner); Luke 15:11–31 (parable of the father and his two sons); Luke 16:1–13 (parable of the dishonest manager).

[18] Elisabeth Schüssler Fiorenza, *In Memory of Her: A Feminist Theological Reconstruction of Christian Origins* (London: SCM, 1983), p. 263.

[19] Kraemer, *Her Share of the Blessings*, p. 50.

[20] David Bentley Hart, *Atheist Delusions* (New Haven and London: YUP, 2009), p. 114.

[21] At least from the sixties, Alan Kreider, *The Change of Conversion and the Origin of Christendom* (Eugene, OR: Wipf & Stock, 1999), p. 13.

[22] Kreider, *Change of Conversion*, p. 39.

[23] The view of the pagan Caecilius recorded by Minucius Felix in Octavius, cited in Kreider, *Change of Conversion*, p. 11.

24 Acts 16:15,30–34; 18:8.
25 Whether this is an approach that has biblical warrant is another matter. A good discussion is provided by Marianne Meye Thompson who states, 'Strikingly, in all the Bible's presentation of God in the "masculine" imagery of Father, God is never held up as the model for "masculinity" for a father or a male over against a mother or a woman. Rather, the way in which God is understood to act obligates human beings in their relationships to each other. The implications of God's Fatherhood are not drawn out for fathers, but for those who wish to live together in the community which God calls into being.' Marianne Meye Thompson, *The Promise of the Father: Jesus and God in the New Testament* (Louisville, KY: Westminster John Knox Press, 2000), p. 182.
26 John 15:12–15. Chapter 7 explores the notion of friendship in the ancient world – its use within the system of patronage, which Jesus subverts.
27 Mark 9:33–7.
28 Luke 12:15; 18:24–5.
29 Matt. 8:21–2.
30 Good, *Jesus' Family Values*, pp. 63–89.
31 Matt. 23:9.
32 Matt. 25:31–46.
33 Fiorenza, *In Memory of Her*, p. 151.
34 Cited in Ruether, *Christianity and the Making of the Modern Family*, p. 33. Celsus' words are preserved in Origen's written response, entitled *Contra Celsum*, to Celsus's criticisms.
35 Acts 2:17.
36 Acts 1:11; 1 Thess. 4:15–17.
37 1 Cor. 7:1–40.
38 1 Cor. 7:3–5.
39 1 Cor. 7:2,8–9.
40 1 Cor. 7:36–8.
41 1 Cor. 7:32–4.
42 1 Cor. 7:7,29,38,40.
43 1 Cor. 7:10–13.
44 1 Cor. 7:21–2. Kenneth Bailey sees in these verses encouragement to slaves to be sure of a calling in Christ despite their circumstances, rather than an endorsement of slavery itself. Kenneth E. Bailey, *Paul Through Mediterranean Eyes: Cultural Studies in 1 Corinthians* (London: SPCK, 2011), pp. 219–20.

45 1 Cor. 7:17,20,24.

46 1 Cor. 7:26.

47 1 Cor. 7:29–31.

48 Fiorenza, *In Memory of Her*, p. 224.

49 Cohick, *Women in the World of the Earliest Christians*, p. 71.

50 Fiorenza, *In Memory of Her*, p. 225.

51 Peter Robert Lamont Brown, *The Body and Society: Men, Women, and Sexual Renunciation in Early Christianity* (New York: Columbia UP, 1988), p. 32.

52 Ruether, *Christianity and the Making of the Modern Family*, p. 38.

53 Col. 3:18 – 4:1.

54 Eph. 5:21 – 6:9. Some Bible translations begin this section not at v. 21 – 'Be subject to one another out of reverence for Christ', but at v. 22 with the comment to wives to be subject to their husbands. However, v. 22 lacks the verb 'subject/submit'; this is inferred from the preceding phrase which states that believers should be subject to one another.

55 1 Pet. 2:18 – 3:7. See also Chapter 5, footnote 49.

56 Edwin Arthur Judge, *The Social Pattern of the Christian Groups in the First Century* (Tyndale Press: London, 1960), p. 28.

57 1 Pet. 2:11–17.

58 1 Tim. 2:1–2.

59 1 Tim. 1:2.

60 1 Tim. 6:14–15.

61 Elsa Tamez, *Struggles for Power in Early Christianity: A Study of the First Letter to Timothy*. trans. Gloria Kinsler (Maryknoll, NY: Orbis, 2007 [2005]), p. 70. She also points out that Timothy is encouraged to stand firm in the faith with reference to how Jesus appeared before Pilate – the man in charge of the occupying forces that controlled the Judean province (1 Tim. 6:13–14).

62 1 Tim. 2:9–14.

63 1 Tim. 3:1–13. In context, the term in v. 11 translated women most likely signifies women deacons. See further below on the evidence for women deacons in the early church.

64 1 Tim. 5:3–16.

65 From *Politics* cited in Fiorenza, *In Memory of Her*, p. 255.

66 Oppian law restricted the amount of gold owned by women and curtailed luxuries like expensive dress and transportation. The law was repealed, argued for by tribune Valerius, saying: 'Give the women

their baubles. These will satisfy their trivial minds and keep them from interfering in more serious matters.' Cited in Ruth A. Tucker and Walter L. Liefeld, *Daughters of the Church: Women and Ministry from New Testament Times to the Present* (Grand Rapids, MI: Academie Books, 1987), p. 55.

67 Cited in Fiorenza, *In Memory of Her*, pp. 232–4.

68 Cited in Tucker and Liefeld, *Daughters of the Church*, p. 76.

69 John Howard Yoder, *The Politics of Jesus* (Grand Rapids, MI: Eerdmans, 1972), pp. 170–83.

70 Yoder, *The Politics of Jesus*, p. 172 (italics in the original). See also footnote 44 above.

71 See also footnote 54 above.

72 Yoder, *The Politics of Jesus*, pp. 180–82.

73 Hence, forbidding marriage (1 Tim. 4:3) was a mark of falsehood rather than an appropriate response to eschatological hopes, in comparison to Paul, himself unmarried, encouraging people not yet married to remain single.

74 1 Cor. 9:19–23.

75 Bruce, *The Epistle of Paul to the Galatians*, p. 190.

76 Yoder, *The Politics of Jesus*, p. 178.

77 Acts 2:17–18.

78 Acts 8:3.

79 1 Tim. 2:9–14, which I return to in Chapter 6 and offer an alternative reading; Titus 2:3–5.

80 Rom. 16:3–4; Acts 18:26.

81 Elisabeth Schüssler Fiorenza, *The Power of the Word: Scripture and the Rhetoric of Empire* (Minneapolis: Fortress Press, 2007), pp. 82–109.

82 Fiorenza, *The Power of the Word*, p. 103.

83 1 Cor. 15:5–7; 12:27–31.

84 Ute E. Eisen, *Women Officeholders in Early Christianity* (Collegeville, MN: Liturgical Press, 2000), pp. 50–51.

85 Eisen, *Women Officeholders*, p. 47.

86 Eisen, *Women Officeholders*, p. 54. 1 Cor. 4:9; Gal. 1:1,11–12.

87 Luke 2:36; 1:41–55; Acts 21:9.

88 Cited in Eisen, *Women Officeholders*, p. 71.

89 Rom. 16:1–2.

90 John Wijngaards, *Women Deacons in the Early Church: Historical Texts and Contemporary Debates* (New York: Crossroad, 2006), pp. 45–6.

91 Eisen, *Women Officeholders*, p. 159.

92 The Latin term *ministrae*, thought to be the equivalent of the Greek *diakonos*, used of these women, subsequently came to be used for deaconesses. It was also used to designate pagan cult officers.

93 Margaret Y. MacDonald, *Early Christian Women and Pagan Opinion: The Power of the Hysterical Woman* (Cambridge: CUP, 1996), p. 51.

94 Anne Jensen, *God's Self-Confident Daughters: Early Christianity and the Liberation of Women* (Kampen, The Netherlands: Kok Pharos, 1996), p. 60.

95 1 Tim. 5:10.

96 Anne Jenson observes that 'clergy' means share of the inheritance; the early church usage of clergy included all those who were paid by the church, Jensen, *God's Self-Confident Daughters*, pp. 22–3.

97 Eisen, *Women Officeholders*, p. 145.

98 This portioning is prescribed in the *Didascalia*; in 1 Tim. 5:16–18 elders receive double the honour or honorarium of recognised widows.

99 Ross Shepard Kraemer argues that the Christian ascetic option for bodily self-control through celibacy and non-marriage created tension with traditional male control over women that the orders of widows and the increasing male regulation of these sought to re-establish. She suggests it is 'no accident that there were no orders of Christian wives'. Kraemer, *Her Share of the Blessings*, p. 196.

100 Eisen, *Women Officeholders*, p. 149–52.

101 Margaret Y. MacDonald, 'Was Celsus Right? The Role of Women in the Expansion of Early Christianity', in *Early Christian Families in Context: An Interdisciplinary Dialogue* (ed. David L. Balch and Carolyn Osiek; Grand Rapids, MI: Eerdmans, 2003), pp. 170–1.

102 MacDonald, 'Was Celsus Right?', p. 184.

103 Rodney Stark, *The Rise of Christianity: How the Obscure, Marginal Jesus Movement Became the Dominant Religious Force in the Western World in a Few Centuries* (San Francisco: Harper Collins, 1997), pp. 95–128. He also states that an argument can reasonably be made that some Christian women therefore married pagans, and that rather than this leading these wives to abandon Christianity, many of their husbands became secondary converts, with their children being raised in the church.

104 Eisen, *Women Officeholders*, pp. 93–100.

105 Eisen, *Women Officeholders*, p. 94.

106 Tucker and Liefeld, *Daughters of the Church*, p. 94.

107 The arguments which were used for this were derived from female subordination and from Jesus' choice of men to baptize him and to be his apostles.

[108] Brown, *Body and Society*, p. 142.

[109] Fiorenza, *In Memory of Her*, p. 286.

[110] Christine Trevett, 'Gender, Authority and Church History: A Case Study of Montanism', *Feminst Theology* (1998): p. 13.

[111] Trevett, 'Gender, Authority and Church History', p. 14.

[112] Kraemer, *Her Share of the Blessings*, p. 157.

[113] Kraemer, *Her Share of the Blessings*, p. 168.

[114] Fiorenza, *In Memory of Her*, p. 303.

[115] Brown, *Body and Society*, pp. 143–4.

[116] Eusebius, *Proof of the Gospel* 1:48–9, http://www.ccel.org/ccel/pearse/morefathers/files/eusebius_de_03_book1.htm (accessed 8 May 2010).

[117] Acts 17:1–9.

3. The Gender Order of Christendom

[1] Diarmaid MacCulloch, *A History of Christianity: The First Three Thousand Years* (London: Allen Lane, 2009), p. 365.

[2] At the time of writing (before the July 2014 General Synod of the Church of England), the existing accommodation (around women's admission to the priesthood) is expressed in the 1993 Act of Synod. Also at the time of writing, the proposed accommodation (concerning the admission of women to the episcopate) is expressed in a self-binding declaration by the House of Bishops that is an undertaking to consider, in the exercise of their episcopal oversight of priests and congregational appointments, the expressed convictions of priests and parishes who do not support the ordination of women, and this would be in place of the 1993 Act of Synod. This declaration would be subject to a disputes resolution process that would hold bishops to account on this matter.

[3] Roland H. Bainton, *Christian Attitudes to War and Peace* (London: Hodder & Stoughton, 1961), pp. 77–8; Alvin John Schmidt, *Veiled and Silenced: How Culture Shaped Sexist Theology* (Macon, GA: Mercer UP, 1989), p. 23.

[4] Bainton, *Christian Attitudes to War and Peace*, pp. 67–8.

[5] Bainton, *Christian Attitudes to War and Peace*, pp. 70–72.

[6] Schmidt, *Veiled and Silenced*, p. 22.

[7] Alan Kreider, *The Change of Conversion and the Origin of Christendom* (Eugene, OR: Wipf & Stock, 1999), p. 23.

8 Schmidt, *Veiled and Silenced*, p. 23.

9 Schmidt, *Veiled and Silenced*, p. 23.

10 Bainton, *Christian Attitudes to War and Peace*, p. 73.

11 Schmidt, *Veiled and Silenced*, p. 23.

12 David L. Dungan, *Constantine's Bible: Politics and the Making of the New Testament* (London: SCM Press, 2006), p. 94.

13 Cited in Kreider, *Change of Conversion*, p. 50.

14 Cited in Schmidt, *Veiled and Silenced*, p. 24.

15 MacCulloch, *History of Christianity*, p. 199.

16 Dungan, *Constantine's Bible*, p. 102–3.

17 Dungan, *Constantine's Bible*, p. 114.

18 Dungan, *Constantine's Bible*, p. 102.

19 Peter Robert Lamont Brown, *The Body and Society: Men, Women, and Sexual Renunciation in Early Christianity* (New York: Columbia UP, 1988), p. 64.

20 Dungan, *Constantine's Bible*, pp. 56,124. Celsus was a pagan critic writing towards the end of the second century.

21 While Christians were not in power, the anti-Jewish stance they adopted did nothing to mitigate against the negative political ramifications being experienced by the Jews at this time (Dungan, *Constantine's Bible*, pp. 81–3).

22 Gnosticism consisted of a dualism between the spiritual and the material. In gnostic thought, the created world was evil and totally separate from and opposite to the world of the spirit. Some gnostic ideas are explored further in Chapter 6.

23 Dungan, *Constantine's Bible*, pp. 57–60.

24 Dungan, *Constantine's Bible*, p. 124.

25 Dungan, *Constantine's Bible*, p. 125.

26 Dungan, *Constantine's Bible*, p. 79.

27 MacCulloch, *History of Christianity*, p. 212.

28 Cited in Kreider, *Change of Conversion*, p. 39.

29 Dungan, *Constantine's Bible*, p. 8.

30 Gary Macy, *The Hidden History of Women's Ordination: Female Clergy in the Medieval West* (New York: OUP, 2008).

31 Extant occurrences of the term presbyterae clearly refer at times to the wives of priests who themselves may have been ordained to a celibate and separated life in support of their husbands' ministries, but also receiving an ordination to their own service in the church. A tenth-century letter by Bishop Atto of Vercelli stating that the church

no longer allows presbyterae refers back to the practice of the early church in which, because of a shortage of male workers, women were ordained to help lead worship, assuming their office by preaching, commanding or teaching. See Macy, *Hidden History of Women's Ordination*, Ch. 3.

[32] The five extant references to episcopae include both those that clearly relate to wives of bishops and women who are not married to bishops. Gary Macy notes that what the references may have in common is that the women were involved in administering church property. See the discussion in Macy, *Hidden History of Women's Ordination*, Ch. 3.

[33] Macy, *Hidden History of Women's Ordination*, p. 110.

[34] The practice of the Orthodox Church today builds on the rulings of this synod, with only monks appointed as bishops in order to avoid the expulsion of wives. Uta Ranke-Heinemann, *Eunuchs for the Kingdom of Heaven: The Catholic Church and Sexuality* (London: Penguin, 1990), p. 106.

[35] Ranke-Heinemann, *Eunuchs for the Kingdom of Heaven*, p. 107.

[36] Rosemary Radford Ruether, *Christianity and the Making of the Modern Family* (London: SCM Press, 2001), p. 50.

[37] Conrad Leyser, 'Custom, Truth, and Gender in Eleventh-Century Reform', in *Gender and Christian Religion* (ed. R.N. Swanson; Woodbridge, Suffolk: Boydell & Brewer, 1998), p. 78.

[38] Ruth A. Tucker and Walter L. Liefeld, *Daughters of the Church: Women and Ministry from New Testament Times to the Present* (Grand Rapids, MI: Academie Books, 1987), pp. 132–7.

[39] Synod of Nimes in 394.

[40] Pope Gelasius' letter to the bishops of Lucania in 494, cited in Ranke-Heinemann, *Eunuchs for the Kingdom of Heaven*, p. 132.

[41] Pope Zachary in 747, cited in Macy, *Hidden History of Women's Ordination*, p. 62.

[42] Snyod of Paris in 829 cited in Ranke-Heinemann, *Eunuchs for the Kingdom of Heaven* p. 133.

[43] Ninth century manuscript, Ranke-Heinemann, *Eunuchs for the Kingdom of Heaven*, p. 133.

[44] Ranke-Heinemann, *Eunuchs for the Kingdom of Heaven*, p. 100.

[45] Ranke-Heinemann, *Eunuchs for the Kingdom of Heaven*, p. 100.

[46] Macy, *Hidden History of Women's Ordination*, p. 115.

[47] Macy, *Hidden History of Women's Ordination*, p. 121.

48 The level of literacy was a determining factor for many in how they might engage in Bible reading and forms of theological learning. The Radical Reformation's emphasis on the independent activity of the Holy Spirit in interpreting the Bible meant that 'a spirit-filled, illiterate, or semi-literate woman or man would be a truer exegete of Scripture than would a learned professor lacking the Spirit'. C. Arnold Snyder and Linda A. Huebert Hecht, eds. *Profiles of Anabaptist Women: Sixteenth Century Reforming Pioneers* (Waterloo, ON, Canada: Wilfrid Laurier UP, 1996), p. 3. Initially before it was curtailed, some women of the Radical Reformation (in a similar way to that of Catholic women mystics, the women in the New Prophecy or the Montanists, and women in the first churches before them) exercised prophetic, teaching and (certainly informal) leadership roles on the basis of pneumatic experience. 'In general, it seems, only the work of the Spirit could disrupt the order that regulated gender relations in church and society!' Kirsi Stjerna, *Women and the Reformation* (New York: Wiley-Blackwell, 2009), p. 15.

49 Lyndal Roper, ' "The Common Man", "the Common Good", "Common Women": Gender and Meaning in the German Reformation Commune', *Social History* 12 (1987): p. 15.

50 Diarmaid MacCulloch, *Reformation: Europe's House Divided 1490–1700* (London: Penguin, 2004), p. 661.

51 Merry E. Wiesner, *Women and Gender in Early Modern Europe* (Cambridge: CUP, 2nd edn, 2000), p. 28 (italics in the original).

52 Wiesner, *Women and Gender*, p. 307.

53 MacCulloch, *Reformation*, p. 610.

54 Karen Armstrong, *The Gospel According to Women* (London: Fount 1986), p. 57.

55 Margaret Aston, 'Segregation in Church', in *Studies in Church History Volume 27: Women in the Church* (ed. W.J. Sheils and Diana Wood; Oxford: Basil Blackwell, 1990), pp. 242, 244. She traces the practice in worship settings of segregating the sexes throughout the Middle Ages, first from east to west which in due course became a north/south division.

56 Linda Woodhead, 'Sex and Secularization', in *Queer Theology: Rethinking the Western Body* (ed. Gerard Loughlin; Oxford: Blackwell, 2007), p. 230.

57 Woodhead, 'Sex and Secularization', p. 230.

4. Equality: A More Just Hermeneutics

[1] The first part of his work appeared in 1791, the second the following year.

[2] The First World War caused a re-examination of voting entitlements. While property qualifications had been lowered for men, they had not been abolished and hence only about 58 per cent of the male population could vote, excluding many of the soldiers and sailors who had served their country. Women's active role during the First World War (doing men's jobs, running their homes, feeding the nation, and generally supporting the war effort), which directly confronted many traditional notions about women, also led to a reappraisal of their right to vote. Angela Holdsworth, *Out of the Doll's House* (London: BBC Books, 1988), p. 186.

[3] Holdsworth, *Out of the Doll's House*, p. 181.

[4] Women sat in the House of Lords for the first time only in 1958 following provisions in the 1958 Life Peerage Act in which life peerages for women and men were created. Hereditary peeresses took their seats for the first time in 1963.

[5] Twinning is used in single-member constituencies under a 'first past the post' voting system. Neighbouring seats are paired taking into account their 'winnability'. Each pair selects one man and one woman by the members of the two constituencies selecting the candidates together, each member voting for one man and one woman. The top man and the top woman are selected and decide between them who should contest which seat.

[6] Zipping is used where there are regional lists with a proportional voting system. In this case women and men are alternated on the lists of candidates.

[7] Equal Opportunities Commission Press Release, 10 March 2001.

[8] In the run-up to the 1997 general election, the Labour Party adopted a policy of all-women shortlists for a number of constituencies. A male party member challenged this practice by making a case of sexual discrimination to an industrial tribunal. The tribunal upheld his case. The Equal Opportunities Commission took further legal advice and this concluded that the selection of candidates fell outside the terms of the Sex Discrimination Act. Ambiguities around the validity of all-women short lists were resolved with the 2002 Sex Discrimination (Elections) Act that made it legal for political parties to use all-women shortlists.

9 Claire Annesley and Francesca Gains, 'The Core Executive: Gender, Power and Change'. *Political Studies* 58 (2010): p. 921.

10 From 7 November. In the private sector the pay gap is 19.9 per cent, while it is 13.6 per cent in the public sector. http://www.tuc.org.uk/equality-issues/gender-equality/equal-pay/women-still-earn-£5000-year-less-men (accessed 17 Nov. 2013).

11 Katherine Rake and Rowena Lewis, *Just Below the Surface: Gender Stereotyping, the Silent Barrier to Equality in the Modern Workplace?* (London, Fawcett Society, 2009), p. 4, http://www.fawcettsociety.org.uk/documents/Just%20Below%20the%20Surface.pdf (accessed 12 Oct. 2009).

12 Jessica Woodroffe, *Not Having It All: How Motherhood Reduces Women's Pay and Employment Prospects* (London, Fawcett Society, 2009), p. 3 http://www.fawcettsociety.org.uk/documents/NotHavingItAll.pdf (accessed 3 Dec. 2010).

13 Jacky Fleming, *Be a Bloody Train Driver* (London: Penguin, 1991), p. 59.

14 'Greater Expectations: Summary Final Report, EOC's investigation into pregnancy discrimination', Equal Opportunities Commission, June 2005.

15 See the information on the British Association for Women in Policing website at http://www.bawp.org/Default.aspx?pageId=1255768 (accessed 17 Nov. 2013).

16 Margaret Gibbon, *Feminist Perspectives on Language* (London and New York: Longman, 1999), p. 62.

17 Gibbon, *Feminist Perspectives on Language*, p. 92.

18 Bonnie J. Miller-McLemore, *Also a Mother: Work and Family as Theological Dilemma* (Nashville, TN: Abingdon Press, 1994), p. 82.

19 Kay Leigh Hagan, 'Introduction', in *Women Respond to the Men's Movement* (ed. Kay Leigh Hagan; San Francisco: Pandora, 1992), p. xiii.

20 Robert Bly, *Iron John: A Book About Men* (Reading, MA: Addison-Wesley, 1990).

21 Rosemary Radford Ruether, 'Patriarchy and the Men's Movement: Part of the Problem or Part of the Solution?' in *Women Respond to the Men's Movement* (ed. Kay Leigh Hagan; San Francisco: Pandora, 1992), pp. 15–16.

22 Margaret Randall, '"And So She Walked over and Kissed Him . . ." Robert Bly's Men's Movement', in *Women Respond to the Men's Movement* (ed. Kay Leigh Hagan; San Francisco: Pandora, 1992), p. 145.

23 See further on pp. 94–95.

24 http://www.whiteribbon.ca/about_us/ (accessed 8 Dec. 2010).

25 http://www.whiteribbon.ca/who-we-are/ (accessed 24 Feb. 2014).

26 See http://www.whiteribboncampaign.co.uk/

27 Stephen B. Boyd, W. Merle Longwood, and Mark W. Muesse, 'Men, Masculinity and the Study of Religion', in *Redeeming Men, Religions and Masculinities* (ed. Stephen B. Boyd, W. Merle Longwood and Mark W. Muesse; Louisville, KY: Westminster John Knox Press, 1996), p. xvii.

28 Consists of full- and part-time stipendiary clergy, and self-supporting ministers, including ordained local ministers.

29 Archbishops' Council, 'Statistics for Mission, 2012: Ministry' (Archbishops' Council, Research and Statistics, Central Secretariat: London, 2013) http://www.churchofengland.org/media/1868964/ministry%20statistics%20final.pdf (accessed 18 November 2013).

30 http://www.cvmen.org.uk/for-women.html (accessed 22 June 2010).

31 http://www.promisekeepers.org/about (accessed 30 Sept. 2010).

32 Patrick Morley, 'The Next Christian Men's Movement', *Christianity Today* (2000) http://www.christianitytoday.com/ct/2000/september4/6.84.html?start=1 (accessed 15 Dec. 2010).

33 Joseph Gelfer, 'Identifying the Catholic Men's Movement'. *Journal of Men's Studies* 16 (2008): p. 46.

34 Cited in Becky Beal, 'The Promise Keepers' Use of Sport in Defining "Christlike" Masculinity'. *Journal of Sport and Social Issues* 21 (1997): pp. 274–84, p. 277.

35 http://www.cmn.org.uk/index.html (accessed 27 Sept. 2010).

36 Edwin Louis Cole, *Maximized Manhood* (New Kensington, PA: Whitaker House, 1982); Patrick Arnold, *Wildmen, Warriors and Kings* (New York: Crossroad, 1991); John Eldredge, *Wild at Heart: Discovering the Secret of a Man's Soul* (Nashville, TN: Thomas Nelson, 2001); Thomas Hughes, *The Manliness of Christ* (London: Macmillan, 1879); S.S. Pugh, *Christian Manliness: A Book of Examples and Principles for Young Men* (London: Religious Tract Society, 1867).

37 The combination of this idea of oppositeness with the notion of the male as norm means gender difference is not about how women and men are different from each other, but how women differ from men. Difference is something belonging to femaleness, not maleness. Put another way, women are 'the other'.

38 Jane Shaw, 'Gender and the Act of Synod', in *Act of Synod – Act of Folly?* (ed. Monica Furlong; London: SCM, 1998), pp. 14–26.

39 These are the terms used by Willard M. Swartley, *Slavery, Sabbath, War and Women: Case Issues in Biblical Interpretation* (Scottdale, PA: Herald Press, 1983).

40 For example, the former is used by the Council for Biblical Manhood and Womanhood (www.cbmw.org) and the latter by Christians for Biblical Equality (www.cbeinternational.org).

41 Mary Stewart Van Leeuwen, 'Servanthood or Soft Patriarchy?', *Priscilla Papers* 11 (1997): pp. 28–40.

42 Melanie Heath, 'Soft-Boiled Masculinity: Renegotiating Gender and Racial Ideologies in the Promise Keepers Movement', *Gender & Society* 17 (2003): pp. 423–44.

43 Arlene Stein, 'Make Room for Daddy: Anxious Masculinity and Emergent Homophobias in Neopatriarchal Politics', *Gender & Society* 19 (2005): pp. 601–20.

44 S. Gallagher and C. Smith cited in Joseph Gelfer, 'Evangelical and Catholic Masculinities in Two Fatherhood Ministries', *Feminist Theology* 19 (2010): p. 41.

45 Judith Stacey and Susan Gerard, cited in Heath, 'Soft-Boiled Masculinity', p. 438.

46 Linda Woodhead, 'Sex and Secularization', in *Queer Theology: Rethinking the Western Body* (ed. Gerard Loughlin; Oxford: Blackwell, 2007), p. 231.

47 Gelfer, 'Evangelical and Catholic Masculinities', p. 50f.

48 http://www.cmn.org.uk/index.html (accessed 27 Sep. 2010).

49 Guy Donegan-Cross, *Men and God* (Cambridge: Grove, 2000), pp. 16–17.

50 Donegan-Cross, *Men and God*, p. 17.

51 Terms frequently used by one Promise Keepers' leader as cited in Becky Beal, 'The Promise Keepers' Use of Sport in Defining "Christlike" Masculinity', 21 (1997): pp. 274–84.

52 Richard Rohr and Joseph Martos say their 1992 book, *The Wild Man's Journey* 'is not for women. Nor is it for softies, wimps or nerds who intend to stay that way for the rest of their lives', cited in Gelfer, 'Identifying the Catholic Men's Movement', p. 44f.

53 Rebecca Merrill Groothuis and Douglas Groothuis, 'Women Keep Promises, Too!', *Priscilla Papers* 11 (1997): p. 4.

54 There are two further protected characteristics of negative duties covered in the Equality Act 2010: pregnancy and maternity, and marriage and civil partnership.

55 The aim of equal opportunity, through removing discriminatory barriers or offering measures to combat disadvantage, is to enable individuals to achieve through their own merits and efforts.

56 Marcia Y. Riggs, 'Equality', in *Dictionary of Feminist Theologies* (ed. Letty M. Russell and J. Shannon Clarkson; London: Mowbray, 1996), pp. 84–5.

57 Equality and Human Rights Commission, 'Working Better: Fathers, Family and Work - Contemporary Perspectives' *Research Summary* 41 (Manchester: EHRC, 2009), p. 10.

58 Starhawk, 'A Men's Movement I Can Trust', in *Women Respond to the Men's Movement* (ed. Kay Leigh Hagan; San Francisco: Pandora, 1992), p. 29.

59 The Universal Declaration of Human Rights states that 'All human beings are born free and equal in dignity and rights. They are endowed with reason and conscience and should act towards one another in a spirit of brotherhood'. Article 1. http://www.un.org/Overview/rights.html (accessed 20 Apr. 2007).

60 When I was researching women's lives in Northern Ireland it became apparent that the idea that women bear a secondary image of God still has an influence in a number of more conservative Christian groupings, at least on some middle-aged and older women who learnt this directly when young. At that time there were still women for whom the idea of their spiritual equality before God was either relatively new or even yet unheard. Fran Porter, *Changing Women, Changing Worlds: Evangelical Women in Church, Community and Politics* (Belfast: Blackstaff, 2002), p. 132–3.

5. Women, Men and Theological Imaginings

1 The words of a 3-year-old girl correcting her mother's female language for God: 'No, that's not right. God is a he. God is a word for boys.' Jann Aldredge Clanton, *In Whose Image? God and Gender* (London: SCM, 1990), p. 75.

2 A girl cited in Anne Phillips, *The Faith Lives of Girls: Children's Spirituality and Transition to Adulthood* (Farnham, Ashgate, 2011), p. 132.

3 1 Cor. 13:12.

4 Deut. 32:18; Pss 18:2; 27:1; 121:5.

5 Linda Hogan, *Human Rights* (Dublin and London: Trocaire; Veritas; and CAFOD, 1998), p. 22.

6 Mary Daly, *Beyond God the Father* (London: Women's Press, 1986), p. 19.

7 Examples from Casey Miller and Kate Swift cited in Dale Spender, *Man Made Language* (London: Pandora, 2nd edn, 1994), p. 156.

8 Example from Elaine Morgan cited in Spender, *Man Made Language*, p. 152.

9 Spender, *Man Made Language*, p. 157 (italics in the original).

10 Spender, *Man Made Language*, p. 154 (italics in the original).

11 Some of the material in this section originally appeared in Fran Porter, *It Will Not Be Taken Away from Her: A Feminist Engagement with Women's Christian Experience* (London: DLT, 2004), Ch. 2.

12 Elizabeth A. Johnson, *She Who Is: The Mystery of God in Feminist Theological Discourse* (New York: Crossroad, 1997), pp. 4–5.

13 Clanton, *In Whose Image?* p. 91.

14 Beverley Clack, 'The Denial of Dualism: Thealogical Reflections on the Sexual and the Spiritual', *Feminist Theology* 10 (1995): pp. 105–6.

15 Johnson, *She Who Is*, p. 35.

16 This includes the use of male personal pronouns to refer to God.

17 Gail Ramshaw, 'The Gender of God', in *Feminist Theology: A Reader* (ed. Ann Loades; London: SPCK, 1990), p. 169.

18 Brian Wren, *What Language Shall I Borrow? God Talk in Worship: A Male Response to Feminist Theology* (London: SCM, 1989), p. 124.

19 Acts 7:54 – 8:3.

20 Acts 9:4–5.

21 Eusebius cited in Ruth A. Tucker and Walter L. Liefeld, *Daughters of the Church: Women and Ministry from New Testament Times to the Present* (Grand Rapids, MI: Academie Books, 1987), p. 94.

22 Cited in Johnson, *She Who Is*, p. 74.

23 Cited in Mary Catherine Hilkert, 'Key Religious Symbols: Christ and God', *Theological Studies* 56 (1995): p. 345.

24 Johnson, *She Who Is*, pp. 151–2.

25 Julie Clague, 'The Christa: Symbolizing My Humanity and My Pain', *Feminist Theology* 14.1 (2005): pp. 83–108.

26 Clague, 'The Christa'.

27 Julie Clague, 'Interview with Margaret Argyle', *Feminist Theology* 10 (1995): p 59.

28 Clague, 'The Christa', p. 97.

29 Clague, 'Interview', p. 66–7.

30 See Nicola Slee, *Seeking the Risen Christa* (London: SPCK, 2011).

31 http://www.womenundersiegeproject.org/conflicts/profile/bosnia (accessed 15 Nov. 2012).

32 Lisa Isherwood, 'Editorial ', *Feminist Theology* 19 (1998): p.7.

33 Clague, 'Interview', p. 66.

34 Clague 'The Christa', p. 107.

35 Clague 'The Christa', p. 107.

36 Luke 22:42.

37 For example, Catherine Clark Kroeger and Nancy Nason-Clark, *No Place for Abuse: Biblical and Practical Resources to Counteract Domestic Violence* (Downers Grove, IL: InterVarsity Press, 2001), gather world-wide statistics outlining the prevalence of male violence against women, and focus specifically on Christian experiences of and responses to such abuse.

38 These symbols are considered to have been the monogram *chi rho* (the first two Greek letters of the word Christ) which Constantine incor-poroated into his military standard, the *labarum*, which expressed Constantine's twin loyalty to the Christian God and the Unconquered Sun. See Stuart Murray, *Post-Christendom* (Carlisle: Paternoster, 2004), pp. 92–4.

39 Rita Nakashima Brock and Rebecca Ann Parker, *Saving Paradise: How Christianity Traded Love of This World for Crucifixion and Empire* (Boston: Beacon Press, 2008), p. 237.

40 A view that was expressed first in the 830s by Carolingian theologian Paschasius Radbertus and which would become the dominant view.

41 Brock and Parker, *Saving Paradise*, p. 238.

42 Brock and Parker, *Saving Paradise*, p. ix.

43 From an early date, making the sign of the cross was a part of liturgical and everyday practice for Christians. While not viewed principally as a motif of Christ's suffering, the cross was the means of Christ's saving work, an indication of his victory and reign, and signing the cross was a means of appropriating God's blessing and protection.

44 I am grateful to Alan Kreider for the observation that, as Ravenna was the western headquarters for the Byzantine emperors, the lived reality for many of the poor within Christendom would likely have been different to that envisaged in this particular iconography. While the imagery on these panels is a reflection of early Christian imagina-tion, this provides another example of the importance of a post-Chris-tendom hermeneutics of suspicion, which asks questions about the power dynamics hidden in our texts and symbols (see also Chapter 6).

[45] Diarmaid MacCulloch, *A History of Christianity: The First Three Thousand Years* (London: Allen Lane, 2009), p. 179.

[46] Brock and Parker, *Saving Paradise*, p. 258.

[47] Brock and Parker, *Saving Paradise*, p. 238.

[48] Brock and Parker, *Saving Paradise*, p. 270.

[49] Betsy J. Bauman-Martin argues that 1 Peter addresses the situation of Christian wives in households of unbelieving husbands and that the submission the author advocates for them is to the consequences, from their husbands, of the women's Christian faithfulness; to convert to Christian faith itself was an act of disobedience, as well as was engaging in Christian liturgical and ethical practices. Hence, there is no parallel to the circumstances of contemporary situations of abuse, and the verses cannot be an exhortation to contemporary women to subject themselves to abuse. Further, the text itself indicates the women were active in resisting the authority of their husbands (by continuing in their faith), and indeed were encouraged to continue doing so by the author. He encourages them to submit to their subsequent persecution, following the pattern of Jesus who also submitted to the consequences of his disobedience of rulers. Betsy J. Bauman-Martin, 'Women on the Edge: New Perspectives on Women in the Petrine Haustafel', *JBL* 123/2 (1995): pp. 253–79.

[50] The statistics of the extent of violence against women are shocking. The One Billion Rising Campaign (www.onebillionrising.org) launched in 2013 by the global activist movement V-Day (www.vday.org) as part of its work to end violence against women and girls takes its name from the UN statistic that one in three women and girls across the world (one billion women) will be beaten or raped in their lifetime. See also the 2008 United Nations Fact Sheet (DPI/2498) available at: http://www.un.org/en/women/endviolence/pdf/VAW.pdf, (accessed 12 March 2013).

[51] Marjorie Procter-Smith, ' "Reorganizing Victimization": The Intersection between Liturgy and Domestic Violence', in *Christian Perspectives on Sexuality and Gender* (ed. Adrian Thatcher and Elizabeth Stuart; Leominster: Gracewing, 1996), p. 381.

[52] Procter-Smith, 'Reorganizing Victimization', p. 380.

6. Gender Relations and the New Testament

¹ A hermeneutics of suspicion is also alert to the extent to which the text itself reflects the voices of the powerful. Hence Lloyd Pietersen, in considering the narrative of Jephthah's daughter (Judg. 11:29–40) and the witness of lament about her fate and the lack of Yahweh's intervention that it contains, remarks that 'It is outrageous, therefore, that Hebrews can simply name Jephthah as one of the heroes of faith without further comment (Heb.11:32–4).' Lloyd Pietersen, *Reading the Bible after Christendom* (Milton Keynes: Paternoster, 2011), p. 110.

² 1 Cor. 11:2–16; 14:34–5; Eph. 5:22–33; Col. 3:18–19; 1 Tim. 2:8–15; 1 Pet. 3:1–7.

³ Stuart Murray, *The Naked Anabaptist* (Scottdale, PA / Waterloo, Ontario: Herald Press, 2010), p. 68.

⁴ This does not mean that the Old Testament should not be explored as Jewish Scriptures, understanding their import for ancient and inter-testamental Israel; such scholarship is necessary for Christian understanding.

⁵ See pp. 66–67, 75–76, 85.

⁶ Matt. 5:9,6; 22:37–40; 5:44; Luke 12:13–34.

⁷ Mark 8:34.

⁸ Wide-angle reading expands where we look, and at what, for the story of gender, while panoramic reading bears in mind the sweep of New Testament evidence that presents a diverse picture of early Christian life.

⁹ Acts 10:1 – 11:18.

¹⁰ Gal. 2:7–14.

¹¹ Acts 15:36–41.

¹² Col. 4:10; Phlm. 24; 2 Tim. 4:11.

¹³ 1 Cor. 1:10–17.

¹⁴ Phil. 4:2–3; Col. 3:13.

¹⁵ Col. 2:8,20–23; Eph. 4:14; 1 Tim. 1:3–4.

¹⁶ 1 Cor. 5:9 – 6:11; 1 Thess. 1:9; 4:3–8; Phlm. 8–19; Jas 2:1–13.

¹⁷ The seven churches addressed in Revelation are variously dealing particularly with: loss of radical discipleship; persecution; idolatry; esoteric knowledge; loss of witness; marginalization; wealth and power. Pietersen, *Reading the Bible after Christendom*, p. 172.

¹⁸ The way in which contemporary Christian communities might reflect the participatory nature of early church practice is explored in Stuart

and Sian Murray Williams, *Multi-Voiced Church* (Milton Keynes: Paternoster, 2012).

[19] As Lloyd Pietersen states, in the thirteen letters of the Pauline corpus, there is both contingency (as specific situations are addressed) and coherence (as it is the same gospel being applied in the various contexts). Pietersen, *Reading the Bible after Christendom*, p. 154.

[20] Col. 3:15–16.

[21] Eph. 5:1–2.

[22] Luke 2:36; Acts 21:9; 1 Cor. 11:5; Luke 24:10; John 4:28–42; Acts 18:26; Phil. 4:2–3; 2 Tim. 1:5; 3:14–15; Tit. 2:3–5; Luke 8:1–3; Acts 12:12; 16:13–15; Rom. 16:1–5; 1 Cor. 16:19; Col. 4:14.

[23] The dating of the epistle, which is bound up in the question of authorship, is pertinent in discussions about the religious context of the letter, but not, as we shall see below, to the detriment of an alternative reading.

[24] Ian Paul, 'Women, Teaching and Authority', in *Women and Men in Scripture and the Church: A Guide to Key Issues* (ed. Steven Croft and Paula Gooder; Norwich: Canterbury Press, 2013), p. 37.

[25] Acts 19:23–7.

[26] Acts 19:28–9,34.

[27] Elsa Tamez, *Struggles for Power in Early Christianity: A Study of the First Letter to Timothy*, trans. Gloria Kinsler (Maryknoll, NY: Orbis, 2007 [2005]), p. 13.

[28] Popular references often are that 'money is the root of all evil' and not the love of money.

[29] The resonances with gnostic ideas in the letter are one reason some date it much later than Paul, towards the end of the first and the beginning of the second century. However, identifying gnostic influences in the first century is plausible 'so long as we do not imagine that there was in the first century a single definable religious movement called "Gnosticism" with a fixed "creed". "Gnostics" came in all shapes and sizes – the term is no more specific than "New Age" is today, and indeed in some ways the two categories are not dissimilar.' R.T. France, *Women in the Church's Ministry: A Test-Case for Biblical Hermeneutics* (Carlisle, UK: Paternoster Press, 1995), p. 58.

[30] Richard Clark Kroeger and Catherine Clark Kroeger, *I Suffer Not a Woman: Rethinking 1 Timothy 2:11–15 in Light of Ancient Evidence* (Grand Rapids, MI: Baker, 1992), pp. 72–3.

31 Catherine Clark Kroeger, Mary Evans, and Elaine Storkey, eds. *Women's Study New Testament* (London: Marshall Pickering, 1995), p. 439.

32 Linda L. Belleville, '1 Timothy', in *The IVP Women's Bible Commentary*, ed. by Catherine Clark Kroeger and Mary Evans (Downers Grove, IL: InterVarsity Press), p. 738.

33 A useful discussion of the terms used in vv. 9–10 are given in Aída Besançon Spencer, *1 Timothy: A New Covenant Commentary* (Eugene, OR: Cascade, 2013), pp. 54–7.

34 Sharon Hodgin Gritz, *Paul, Women Teachers, and the Mother Goddess at Ephesus: A Study of 1 Timothy 2:9–15 in the Light of the Religious and Cultural Milieu of the First Century* (Lanham, MD: UP of America, 1991), p. 128.

35 The idea that younger women (in comparison to those who are older) may find it hard to remain celibate (1 Tim. 5:11) is not dissimilar to the directions to Christian women and men at Corinth that they should marry if they are unable to practise self-control (1 Cor. 7:9).

36 1 Cor. 14:28,30 regarding women and men (1 Cor. 11:4–5); and also 1 Cor. 14:34 referring to women on their own.

37 Kroeger and Kroeger, *I Suffer Not a Woman*, pp. 75–6 (italics in original).

38 See Kroeger and Kroeger, *I Suffer Not a Woman*, pp. 87–98 for a discussion of possible meanings and ancient usage.

39 Kenneth E. Bailey, 'Women in the New Testament: A Middle Eastern Cultural View', *Theology Matters* 6 (2000): pp. 1–11, p. 9.

40 Paul, 'Women, Teaching and Authority', p. 38.

41 Bailey, 'Women in the New Testament', p. 2.

42 France, *Women in the Church's Ministry*, p. 66.

43 Kroeger and Kroeger, *I Suffer Not a Woman*, pp. 99–104, 189–92.

44 Kroeger and Kroeger, *I Suffer Not a Woman*, p. 103.

45 Richard Clark Kroeger, and Catherine Clark Kroeger argue that 1 Timothy was written at a time when the later gnostic mythology about Eve, Adam and the serpent that we know of was in a formative period, arguing that these later mythologies 'could not have been so widespread without a previous formulative period' (*I Suffer Not a Woman*, p. 119).

46 Kroeger and Kroeger, *I Suffer Not a Woman*, p. 103.

47 Kroeger and Kroeger, *I Suffer Not a Woman*, p. 103.

48 Lynn H Cohick, *Women in the World of the Earliest Christians: Illuminating Ancient Ways of Life* (Grand Rapids, MI: Baker, 2009), pp. 135–6.

[49] There is a view that this whole passage is actually about wives and husbands and how they behave in the setting of Christian worship, placing the import of v. 15 within the context of married couples in the church at Ephesus. David M. Scholer, '1 Timothy 2:9–15 & the Place of Women in the Church's Ministry', in *Women, Authority and the Bible* (ed. Alvera Mickelsen; Basingstoke: Marshall Pickering, 1987), pp. 193–219. See also the brief discussion in France, *Women in the Church's Ministry*, pp. 60–1.

[50] For example, a creative engagement is given in Beverly J. Stratton, 'Eve through Several Lenses: Truth in 1 Timothy 2.8–15', in *A Feminist Companion to the Hebrew Bible in the New Testament* (ed. Athalya Brenner; Sheffield: Sheffield Academic Press), pp. 258–60.

7. Post-Christendom Women and Men

[1] This discretion was permissive not prescriptive in character, and hence did not set a precedent or oblige other bishops to do the same, but was understood as a decision adopted by particular bishops for specific local reasons. All liturgical services (those of lectors, ministers of the word and eucharistic ministers) 'are carried out by lay people . . . according to the judgment of the bishop, without lay people, be they men or women, having any right to exercise them'. Bishops and priests remain under obligation to support 'the noble tradition of altar boys', which had helped encourage priestly vocations. Congregation for Divine Worship and the Discipline of the Sacraments, Letter to the Presidents of Conferences of Bishops Concerning the Liturgical Service of Lay Persons, 15 March 1994: *Notitiae* 30 (1994) pp. 333–5, 347–8.

[2] Fran Porter, *It Will Not Be Taken Away from Her: A Feminist Engagement with Women's Christian Experience* (London: DLT, 2004), p.108.

[3] *Newsnight*, 7 July 2008, see also http://news.bbc.co.uk/1/hi/uk/7494517.stm (accessed 8 May 2013). In January 2011, John Broadhurst was among the first of three former Church of England bishops who, recently having been received into the Roman Catholic Church, were ordained as priests in the Personal Ordinariate of Our Lady of Walsingham. The Ordinariate was established by papal decree of Pope Benedict for groups of Anglican faithful and their pastors within England and Wales wishing to enter into full communion with the

Catholic Church. This was almost two years before the proposals put at the General Synod in November 2012 that would have facilitated the appointment of women as bishops failed to achieve the necessary two thirds majority in the House of Laity.

4   Daphne Hampson, *After Christianity* (London: SCM Press, 1996), p. 77.
5   Elaine Storkey, *The Search for Intimacy* (London: Hodder & Stoughton, 1995), p. 153.
6   John 15:12–17.
7   C.K. Barrett, *The Gospel According to John* (London: SPCK, 2nd edn, 1978), p. 392, considers this probable and in addition to the references in John 15 cites the use of the term in the following places: John 11:11 (where Lazarus is described as our friend or 'a friend of the whole company'); 3 John 13 (which ends with greetings from 'the friends'); Luke 12:4 (where Jesus addresses the disciples as 'my friends'); and Acts 27:3 (which talks of Paul being cared for by his friends in Sidon).
8   Carolyn Osiek and David L. Balch, *Families in the New Testament World: Households and House Churches* (Louisville, KY: Westminster John Knox Press, 1997), p. 48.
9   Luke 8:1–3; Acts 16:14–15,40; Rom. 16:1–2. A full discussion of these women as benefactors of Jesus and the early church is found in Lynn H. Cohick, *Women in the World of the Earliest Christians: Illuminating Ancient Ways of Life* (Grand Rapids, MI: Baker, 2009), pp. 301–9.
10 Peter Atkinson, *Friendship and the Body of Christ* (London: SPCK, 2004), p. 8.
11 Luke 7:34; Matt. 11:19.
12 Mark 14:3–9; Luke 7:36–50.
13 Elizabeth Green, 'More Musings on Maleness: The Maleness of Jesus Revisited', *Feminist Theology* 20 (1999): p. 26.
14 Atkinson, *Friendship*, p. 3.
15 This may also be true when using gender-neutral language for God – removing, for example, the use of 'he', 'him' and 'his'. Sometimes an absence of familiar male God-talk is equally unsettling as the introduction of occasional female imagery.
16 Some approaches to exploring gender-inclusive imaging of the divine project human categories of sexual distinction and gender difference onto deity rather than seeing these as metaphorical vehicles for speaking of God. In doing so, these approaches may continue to reflect and perpetuate dualistic gender relations. These (sometime overlapping) approaches include: ascribing dual gender to God (God

is both female and male); ascribing a dual essentialism to God (God is both feminine and masculine principle); ascribing femininity as well as masculinity to God (associating particular characteristics or metaphors for God along gendered lines); dividing the persons of the Trinity along gender lines (with the Holy Spirit as feminine). It is not that elements within these approaches are not useful or without precedent (for example, there is scriptural warrant for identifying the Spirit through female imagery and for seeing female embodiment and experience as valid and valuable metaphorical allusions). But, as with gender-exclusive imaging of God, projecting human categories of sexual distinction and gender difference onto deity loses sight of the way metaphor functions in imaging the divine.

[17] I use the term prophetic here in the sense of speaking and acting in ways that reveal realities that dominant majorities refuse or are unable to acknowledge.

[18] Mary Stewart Van Leeuwen, ed., *After Eden: Facing the Challenge of Gender Reconciliation* (Grand Rapids, MI, Eerdmans: 1993), p. 344.

[19] Numerous examples of these scenarios are given in Fran Porter, *Changing Women, Changing Worlds: Evangelical Women in Church, Community and Politics* (Belfast: Blackstaff, 2002).

[20] Phil. 2:12.

[21] John W. de Gruchy, *Being Human: Confessions of a Christian Humanist* (London: SCM, 2006), p. 153.